THAT DARLINGTON

The spirit of old High Row

Beryl Hankin
and other people who knew it well

Published by

Guru Boutique

**24 Blackwellgate,
Darlington, DL1 5HG
Tel: 01325 461479
This is a first print 2007**

The King's Head Hotel, Darlington
designed by G.G. Hoskins

Contents

Background

In May 2007 I carried out an independent survey to firstly ascertain the reactions of my fellow townspeople of Darlington to the aesthetic, emotional and cultural changes redevelopment had brought to this traditional town, and secondly to discover if town users were experiencing any problems or benefits in the new central area and whether these problems/benefits balanced each other out. The findings of this survey were handed over to Darlington Borough Council and they must have been helpful, as anyone who read all the useful comments made by people from all sections of our society (including skateboarders, business owners, visitors, shoppers, families, people with disabilities, pensioners and representatives from most walks of life), would be able to form a comprehensive overall picture of the effect this major face change to our town has had on us all. This survey was not a political or business orientated undertaking but was simply done in an effort to help ourselves, our council, our town and the people who have supported it over the years to deal with the effects of the changes.

That part done it seemed to me that in order for some of us to move on, and out of respect for our history, the other necessary thing which had to be attempted was to try and commemorate in some way our former central townscape which had meant so much to so many of us in so many different ways. In order to reach as many people as possible a competition was advertised by us in The Northern Echo and the ensuing responses form the basis of this hopefully worthwhile book.

Beryl Hankin

Even the pidgeons get to appear as after all they are part of High Row
Photo by Rebecca Flynn

Dedication

This book is dedicated to Darlington and to everyone who understood in some way the true spirit of High Row between 1901, when it seems our Victorian forebears completed their version, and 2007 when the current incarnation was finally launched.

High Row c1901 - Copyright The Francis Frith Collection, SP35QP

Darlington is a brilliant and rapidly expanding place with ever improving facilities and continous efforts being made to combat social problems. It is a great town to live in and to visit, and we have people and businesses here which are second to none and I hope the quality of life continues to improve. That said there are enough people who feel like I do, who have a deep affinity for the town and mourn the passing of old High Row and for that reason we cannot let this event pass without comment. I think our town would have been even more satisfactory if it had retained a fully restored High Row, as it still had such a lot to give - and I miss it so much!

B.H.

Message

This message is to anyone who is in a position to influence the policies concerning the future of our built environment.

I doubt such exalted beings will ever read this book as we are only little people in the scheme of things, but are we not the little people in whose name all this current spate of redevelopment is being carried out?

If those with the power to change things do however happen to open these pages I hope that what they see here will enable them to better understand the effects some redevelopments can have on communities and individuals. It is not enough just to leave buildings intact as street patterns are important too and in most cases already blend with and enhance the architecture and atmosphere of a place, so in the course of admittedly necessary resurfacing and adjustments to reflect current needs, it is vital that repaving or alterations to streets and roadways truly represent the taste, continuity, spirit and personal history of the location and the established community they are to serve. I have used as an example Darlington's High Row and some Darlington people's relationships with it, and if our experiences can in some way prevent any further loss of that wonderful British quirkiness and individuality in other town centres (seemingly done all in the name of shopping), our old High Row has not been lost in vain.

Not usually being a very bold person I prefer to keep myself to myself so this is entirely out of character for me, but for once I have broken my own rule and am sticking up for a belief which I regard is a moral duty and my right.

This is only part of this book as whether you feel as I do or not or whether you have involvement in town planning or not, the interesting articles and visuals that all the other people concerned have supplied are definitely worth reading and looking at. I'm sure not all of the contributors have the same views as I do so I am not speaking for them, but they do all have a real connection with Darlington. Don't let my underlying message put you off a comprehensive compilation and a really good read.

I hope you will forgive me on this rare occasion for airing my own deeply felt views and putting out my message, as it has been a difficult thing for me to do and really quite scary…because if most of the old movies I've seen are anything to go by, don't they always shoot the messenger..?

B.H.

Author/compiler of this book

Beryl Hankin has been lucky enough to have had a passion for many things including music, literature, architecture, people, Guru Boutique and her hometown Darlington, for as long as she can remember.

Beryl said...

"I am proud to have been able to compile the contents of 'That Darlington Way (the spirit of old High Row)', and could not have done it without all the fantastic contributions made by everyone featured within its pages. It was decided that we would just go ahead and print this book without the benefit of an editor to sanitize it as we wanted it to be as raw, real and natural as possible so that the emotion could shine through…therefore if we have made a few slip ups please forgive us and we hope you accept and enjoy it in the spirit in which it was intended.

I think it is important to pay tribute to the part of our central townscape which is the subject of this book if only for the following reason. Had you photographed High Row in 1901 when it was newly built, and then revisited the viewpoint from which that shot was taken at any time up to 2006, you could have held that photograph up and seen before you (apart from the changes to motor vehicles and fashions in clothing and some lovely buildings that were sadly demolished probably in the 60's), the very same scene preserved almost exactly in real life, as the one you were looking at in the picture you held in your hand. I think that is something very rare and in fact it is almost a miracle that our unique three tiered High Row had managed to survive almost intact for so many years and that marked our town out from all others. It was a completely unique scene and epitomised Darlington and all we stand for, and was a visible reminder of the many momentous and not so momentous events that had taken place on it over the hundred or so years of its existence.

I hope anyone reading this will think we have achieved what we set out to do, which was to capture it's essence in these pages and to show from many viewpoints as many as possible of the things that Darlington means to us, and in so doing touch on not just one aspect but on almost all that this town is about, using only one backdrop (our old High Row) as the narrow setting for a project dealing with such a wide variety of historical, commercial, social and cultural richness. This only highlights what an important part of our town and of our collective consciousness that place has been".

Beryl.

Acknowledgements

Sincere gratitude must go to all who responded to the request for contributions to this project, as everything received was of the highest quality, unfortunately it was just not possible to include everything due to lack of space as there was enough material to fill several volumes.

Special thanks also go to the following:

Ray (my husband) for putting up with all the domestic disruption.

Tony, Colin and Kelly my friends at Guru who had to do my work on many occasions due to me being absorbed in this project.

Allene Norris, Richard Hindle and Tony Smith (our three judges) for putting real thought, time and effort into the monumentally difficult task of judging the competition that preceded this book.

Ann Rider for giving such good help and advice.

Katherine, Brian, Christine, and all the staff of the Centre for Local Studies in Darlington Public Library for all their friendly efficiency in connection with obtaining photographs and news items from the library's archives.

Gary Hall for friendship and the use of some of his wonderful lyrics.

Chris Lloyd for all his excellent books and articles on Darlington.

Bill and JJ for help and music.

Lauren Pyrah for her professionalism.

Ellen Dean for humour and advice.

Jilly Penegar and Lesley Cardwell for help and friendship.

Colin Bainbridge for help with old photographs.

The Frith Gallery for help with old photographs.

Bridget Emmerson and G. Prudhoe & Co Ltd for old postcards.

Dulcie Noble for introducing us to Joan Wright.

Rodney Burges for introducing us to Bill Lawson.

Hugh Mortimer (Mort) for information and photographs.

Ray Davies for being a champion of British quirkiness and real life everywhere.

Ian Siegal and Ray Lamontagne for the music which sort of kept me sane.

Mike Sanchez, Al Gare, Mark Mason and Oliver Darling for being one of the best rock'n'roll bands in the history of this planet.

Stuart, Mark and all at SD Print for infinite patience and for achieving so well the formidable task of making the appearance of 'That Darlington Way' turn out just as we all hoped it would.

Darlington
This was then ... and that is now

created by Lee Hutchinson of Evolva

This is a picture taken in 1910. How poignant it seems that even when modern people are superimposed as they are here, upon such an early image of old High Row they don't seem out of place - surely proof that is was a true classic

"A bow worn in steps
tells of millions of feet
going up from high to low,
year to year the bustle repeats
up to and along High Row...
Layer upon layer we add our lives,
walk through and feel the air..."

extract from 'Spirits in the Stones' by David Thompson

Both ends of the era

Hello 'old' High Row in the early 1900's

Goodbye 'old' High Row in 2006

It is often said that beauty is in the eye of the beholder and I'm quite aware that some, especially those arriving fresh to Darlington will see our 2007 High Row as being perfectly ok. I however miss the thrill of walking on that historic three tiered place and will find it hard to come to terms with the knowledge that it is gone. It is not easy to develop affection for wide utilitarian streets paved to a formula.

The End of an Era

This is all about the end of an era in a Northern town called Darlington. It was my era and that of my parents and my grandparents and it may (depending on age and other aspects) have been your era too. It was a good time in many ways if a difficult one in others. During it Britain has seen wars and peaceful times. Darlington was lucky as it escaped major bomb damage in the Second World War which meant our townscape has seen the decades come and go and remained relatively unchanged in appearance. Some happy memories and remarkable characters emerged from the times people had to live through and there was a sense of continuity which it seemed nothing could dent. The town was a place where people liked to go, not just for shopping or to do business transactions, but as a social centre and a nice place to be and to be seen in. They'd go there to show off a new baby or a new car perhaps, or just to have a walk about or meet up with friends and watch the world go by. The town seemed to have a life and will of its own and evolved gently in its own individual way to accommodate each new demand or challenge the outside world placed upon it as it came along. There was also a sense of personal freedom and pride in belonging here, whatever age or class a person was. This is not so much the case now as in this emerging new era one gets the impression that there is intent to try and force such places into a similar mould and to categorise the people who use them. It almost seems to me that authenticity and individuality is starting to be viewed as not desirable where a town centre is concerned. These previously relaxed, diverse and interesting places which displayed the personality of the community they served are now often regarded simply as "retail offers" to quote the current jargon, and are turning into mere shopping machines where everything is geared up to encourage us to consume, and where banners, barcodes and units rule and something a little bit different doesn't fit in, and where the choices of what we purchase, be it anything from books or music to the clothes we wear and the food we eat, is becoming more and more pre-determined for us by the computerised statistics of the corporate giants. I hope this doesn't come over as being too heavy, but to be honest I don't like to see so many of our unique town centres turning into these bland predictable places, and I feel sorry for the next generations who it appears are already being groomed as potential consumers rather than free willed human beings, as they may not all be allowed the pleasure of developing a loyalty to one particular place as so many towns seem to be becoming very alike. If this trend continues many town centres will soon be almost interchangeable. So yes I like towns, and yes I like shopping trips, and yes I'm all for commercial and social success stories, but more importantly I like those things to take place in a proper town which has its own attractive identity or heritage, and where you can sometimes stumble upon the unexpected. Furthermore a real town as well as being a magnet for tourists, provides stimulation for all sorts of people with imagination enough to appreciate it. It should offer value, choice and variety, allow us to think and decide for ourselves, and be a place where people are treated with the respect they deserve and where there is provision, tolerance, space and time

**The end
of an era**

for all ages and abilities, including the unique amongst us. I have worries that Darlington is following sheep like into a new era which doesn't include as many of those qualities mentioned above as I would like, an era which began for this town in my opinion with the decision to go ahead with the demolition of our old High Row. I truly believe that a town like ours can only compete by being itself and therefore pleasingly different and an influence for good in contrast with the sprawling shopping centre sort of environment which usually at worst encourages certain types of disruptive urban behaviour patterns or at best is just taken for granted as a functional but soulless necessity.

There will be lots of people I'm sure who will totally disagree with all I have said here and I respect their view as I hope they will respect mine and that of all who feel as I do. The reason that I and plenty of other people feel qualified and even obliged to make our feelings public in this book is that in short it matters to us, and I suspect the people who think that we are stupid to let it matter do not share our deep sense of place. I can appreciate it if anyone cannot understand what this means as it would not do if we were all the same, but that does not alter the fact that some of us feel real hurt at the loss our former High Row, a location we treasured so much. We do actually feel passionately about the need to preserve the vitally important authentic images of not just Darlington, but of valued scenes in the countryside, villages, towns and cities throughout the rest of Great Britain as well. I just cannot see in the future artists or photographers wanting to perpetuate a series of identikit town centres in the way their predecessors revelled in depicting townscapes in the past and I think that is a shame. We are known as a nation of shopkeepers and that's ok as I am one myself, but to be known as a nation of shopping malls complete with stylised public art which in the main the public never asked for is a step too far, and one that in many cases once accomplished cannot be reversed. In a way the demands of society itself has caused all this to happen, but I think it is now time for that same society to stop and look at itself and make a few changes to its forward planning.

I must make it clear at this point that my views are not necessarily the views of the other people who have contributed to 'This Darlington Way' who obviously may not all feel exactly the same way as I have stated I do above (and in other places in this publication), but that is precisely the point we hope to make here. Just as we would like a real town to do, this book allows for variety, self expression, free thinking and contains views, anecdotes, surprises, emotions and affection for a place, which have come from people from almost all walks of life. It also includes descriptions of the ends of eras of shops and businesses and even public houses and tries to be (as far as possible) inclusive of the whole of society as young, old, highlife, lowlife, rich, poor, appreciative visitor or proud resident, well educated or still struggling like me, we all in a way belong to this town of Darlington which we love, and it belongs to us. Our old High Row has been used as a symbol of the town, its people and its history for the purposes of this book.

B.H.

Preface

History

The subject under scrutiny here is a manmade place, which was built around 1900 and has been the focal point of a town called Darlington for (just over) 100 years since then. It was until recently a three tiered footpath and roadway design that graced the central area of this market town. It may seem a bit unusual to be producing a book about a street pattern in a medium sized Northern town, as how can anyone get excited about that you may ask? This is not just any street we are talking about here however, it is Darlington's legendary and much loved former High Row, where many memories lay and which, in the form just described, is now gone forever. In case you are not conversant with what has happened to bring about this publication, what follows should put you in the picture. By some happy miracle our town centre had survived almost intact for such a long time that it had become living workable history. For people of all ages it was a privilege and a pleasure to know that when you were in the very special town centre of Darlington, and on the High Row in particular, you were part of a streetscape that had been around for generations and that your distant ancestors had also gazed upon and been part of this very same scene. This was a steadying and comforting feeling for many of us. Then suddenly it was all totally re-developed. It is always painful to see history disappear before one's eyes, especially when that history is embodied in a charming, classic environmental feature which although in need of renovation, had not yet outlived its relevance. Such many believe was the case in Darlington when our town lost its bridge to the past and its legacy for the future, our old High Row which had stood the test of time and was regarded with great affection by so many. On the 1st of July 2007, after nearly two years of upheaval its replacement was complete, and the whole ethos of this once gentle place changed forever.

Community

Almost all will agree that the whole of Darlington town centre was rather run down and well overdue for high quality resurfacing, refurbishing and perhaps pedestrianising, to enhance the amazingly comprehensive range of shops, businesses and facilities we have here. Many of us however, would have favoured a stunning restoration project rather than re-development, but that can never happen now. Darlington, situated in such a brilliant location for road, rail and air access as it is, can't help but attract an influx of new development and population, and that is good. New ways, new ideas and new blood are essentials for healthy future growth in any area of life. The hard part is managing such rapid expansion in a way which is sensitive to and respectful of heritage, so that whilst going forward we don't throw valuable existing assets away. Darlington was already successful on many levels and greatly appreciated by its core businesses and population (and the enthusiastic circle of admirers it attracted from the places surrounding it), many of whom had invested much of their lives and many of their dreams here. The removal of long standing points of reference and sense of place has in some cases been very unsettling for these groups of people. Whether we consciously know it or not, when familiar townscape features are destroyed a lot more than pavements and physical constructions are lost, as part of ourselves are bound up with the built environment we grew up with that shaped not just our lives, but the lives of those who have gone before us as well.

Emotion

We can't turn the clock back and we must move on, so for those of us who are emotionally bound up with this town we hope what follows will help us to do that. Even if you have not contributed words or pictures as long as you are interested enough to give your time to read this compilation it is hoped you will not only relate to what you are about to find in these pages, but also in some way become part of it.

'That Darlington Way' is about feelings, not about making comparisons and simply exists in order to record personal attachments to a place which although attractive and special to a lot of us, was perhaps not even that architecturally notable to the outside world. Nonetheless it was unique, seemingly timeless and was somewhere that only we had, which also looked harmonious and worked beautifully as a safe and useful feature in our sloping town. In their own words a random selection of pre 2007 High Row's many friends who used and enjoyed it, will share their experiences of the old place with all who want to view them, but not in the form of a nostalgic and historical record as that has been done so well already by our many gifted local historians and writers on Darlington, but in a very human, personal, sometimes even irreverent but always affectionate way. Perhaps these writings and images may be useful, to society in general, as they show how varied members of a community used their creativity to deal with a big environmental shock. It's heart warming that people are interested and involved enough in this excellent town to respond as they have, and what they say in those varied responses only goes to show that Darlington inspires people enough to really care. In order for us mere mortals to manage to come to terms with any situation it is first necessary to attempt to truthfully express ourselves, and that is what we have tried to do here.

Summary

We believe that we have managed to put as much as we genuinely feel and know about old High Row as possible (given the confines of space, resources and time), into this book in order to celebrate that lost symbol of our town's identity and all the differing things it meant to us. In short we have tried to put 'our' High Row into a book, and we hope that at least part of its soul will live on entwined with ours, far into the future if only on paper. Our book has been lovingly complied with care, passion and sincerity. We hope its contents will raise awareness, engage, entertain, prove healing and constructive for all concerned, and most importantly truly capture the spirit of old High Row.

All there is to do now is read on, and enjoy the originality and talent of all the people who contributed to this heartfelt communal project.

Coronation Day 1911
Sourced from the Centre for Local Studies in Darlington Public Library

Foreword

Whatever would Joseph Pease have made of it all?

Well Darlington's High Row has certainly seen many things over its hundred or so years. Examples of people being good, bad, hardworking, lazy, proud, humble, courageous, afraid, sober, drunken, ceremonial, silly, gentle, violent, fine, tawdry, happy, sad, living life to the full and even dying lonely deaths have all taken place here, played out under the seemingly watchful eye of the statue which commemorates one of our most historically important citizens the eminent Quaker Joseph Pease.

Joseph Pease was born in 1799 and was educated at a Society of Friends school in London. He married Emma Gurney in 1826 and they had sixteen children together. Joseph helped his father Edward in the Darlington Railway Company and by 1830 was owner of a huge number of collieries in this area. He and other businessmen bought some land on the river Tees and created a port (for the export of Durham coal), which eventually became the successful town of Middlesbrough. In 1832 he became the first Quaker MP in Britain. The Quakers in general were active in the areas of social justice and equality. They believed in the abolition of slavery (Pease supported the campaign in this country), equal rights for women and an end to warfare. Joseph Pease himself became the president of the Peace Society in 1860. In Pease was combined a successful businessman and family man. He was an upright and religious person with a strong sense of duty to his fellow men and his social obligations. This is the character of the man commemorated in the monument that overlooks our High Row. The world and society in general has gone through many changes since he was here, and if he were to return he would probably not

be insulated against the new world he would find. His statue however has no doubt gazed upon many things he would have found unimaginable in his time, and you'll find almost all of these things, defining the highs and the lows, the total folly and the sheer richness of experiences which combine to form the human condition and the life of this town, here in this book. If he could speak through that image of himself which guards over us all I wonder what he would have to say?

Photograph supplied by Mr. John Patrick Walsh

Tony Smith.

Major architects of Darlington and us -

a personal view

In our humble opinion the 'major architects of Darlington' to date are Alfred Waterhouse (1830 - 1905) and George Gordon Hoskins (1837 - 1911), and 'us' are (very obviously) neither professional writers or architects, but just two of the people whose outlook these designers of uplifting buildings have influenced.

A townscape is of necessity an ever evolving and ever changing entity. It is a given that every generation must adapt it for its own use and make its mark upon it. Whilst doing this one hopes that any alterations or new introductions will be carefully executed and that where possible the past meaningful, architectural triumphs of a place are successfully incorporated with new triumphs reflecting the age in which they are added. When the visual and functional aspects of any design combine to produce something which is 'good for the soul' as well as highly user friendly that is a truly worthwhile achievement. Sometimes new buildings are done

The entrance to the former Northgate Technical College designed by G. G. Hoskins (and where incidentally Beryl met Ray)

**Major
architects of
Darlington
and us -**
*a personal
view*

Hilary Heward is the artist of this pen and ink drawing depicting the beautiful Pearl Assurance building which used
to stand on the Bondgate end of High Row, but was lost to us in the late 60's.
Hilary had just left school at the time when she from a photograph in 1978

in a sort of reproduction style to blend in with what is around them and whilst this is preferable to creating something ugly or unsuitable in a formerly traditional area, personally we are of the opinion in the cases of both buildings and public places where it is definitely impossbile to take the ideal course of restoring the original, or where the project is an entirely new one on a previously unoccupied space, then (and I realise this is being naively idealistic as in these days problems with finance, time and sometimes even imagination often prohibit this goal), it is morally and artistically desirable that a bold, groundbreaking, superbly well designed contemporary replacement should be constructed using the technology and materials of the day to celebrate the best of the age it is built in. If done well this should not only tend to enhance the character and appearance of a place, but also form a visually stimulating contrast to the area and buildings in the vicinity. It is perfectly possible for stunning new designs and architecture to fit well with existing classics. The revitalised and exceptional Gateshead/Newcastle upon Tyne Quaysides are striking examples if this, with the wonderfully stylish authentically retro Baltic Art Gallery and the fabulously futuristic Sage music venue creating a memorable harmony on the Gateshead side of the water, successfully linked to the Newcastle side by the clean lined Millennium Winking Eye Bridge, which looks great and makes a pleasing addition to the wonderful older bridges across the river Tyne. The view from

**Major
architects of
Darlington
and us -**
*a personal
view*

either side of that great river (or even along it), is a well thought out harmonious mix of historical and cutting edge architecture, which we think lives together as a perfect blend. Not all towns achieve this however, and there are many instances where lack of vision or not enough attention to detail or indifference to the relationship between new works and exisiting environment, result in glaring mistakes needlessly marring many a grand design. Here in our lovely compact town of Darlington we have had both triumphs for many and regrets for some. We have been privileged to have had our buildings overseen by some brilliant architects and we have also allowed eyesores to spring up on the sites of formerly precious pieces of Darlington and seen the destruction of some of our finest assets, especially in the 1960's. We still have some truly inspiring architecture and we should cherish it as little by little it can so easily be chipped away at in the name of 'economic necessity'. No book about Darlington's townscape worth its salt can be complete without tribute being paid to two of our early outstandingly important architects A Waterhouse and G. G. Hoskins. These men were employed by the eminent Quakers of the time to put their architectural stamp on this town, and they did just that with phenomenal style. It's true they built in the general fashion of the time they lived in, but they also added their own highly unique flair and indisputable understanding of the needs and character of Darlington to all they were involved with and that is what singles out their contributions to the town the most for they provided the individual buildings which combine to define the atmosphere of this place and mark it out from other townscapes created by other architects around the same time. We should be eternally glad that it was these two men, amongst all others in their era, who put their signature on our town. Amongst their greatest achievements are many of the fine private mansions they were commissioned to build in the town at the time and some stunning public buildings. Initially being Waterhouse's commission they were to work together in the early 1860's on that jewel of the High Row Backhouses (now Barclays) Bank, and that memorable project established Hoskins in Darlington. Waterhouse designed for many other places in England whilst Hoskins based himself here in this town of Darlington which he seems to have adopted. Waterhouse is also responsible for the wonderful medieval style town clock, market building and old town hall, which stand opposite High Row and which are a delight to behold, and more than all his other works we think these are the ones the people of Darlington must be the most grateful to him for.

George Gordon Hoskins put his stamp on this town in a big way being the man who in addition to his work on Backhouses Bank, designed amongst other works the following incredibly arresting buildings, The Darlington Public Library, The King's Head Hotel and the former Darlington Technical College in Northgate (he also was responsible for Middlesbrough's fine Town Hall). He had offices in Blackwellgate at one time at a site occupied by Binns now and I believe he was badly injured when an explosion occured in the buildings adjacent. For defining the style of this town in the way he did, he was quite simply a Darlington hero. He was not without trouble however as he was partly blamed for a terrible

Major
architects of
Darlington
and us -
*a personal
view*

local tragedy and probably never recovered from the worry he must have felt as a result of this. In later life his name was given as the architect of our lovely Civic Theatre but it is thought that another architect did most of the work on that most attractive building.

Photo of Barcleys Bank, High Row, Darlington by Colin Bainbridge

Not only Barclays but other banks in the town such as HSBC, Lloyds and Nat West (which sensibly retained its facade whilst being completely refurbished inside), are buildings to be proud of too. There are other earlier notable examples of fine architecture in our town, such as the beautiful and historic St Cuthbert's Church, and indeed most of the church architecture from earlier times (including the building which will shortly be vacated by the Salvation Army) is very pleasing to the eye. On a much more modest scale are some of the older public houses and shops which have been kept in good repair and still retain their interesting original appearances, and we personally enjoy seeing features such as the market cross which underlines our pride in our town's market tradition and other pieces of our history such as fountains, drinking troughs and plaques on walls like the one in Bull Wynd. There is every reason why these should remain as important and educational parts of our town as we progress into a viable commercial future. We think our former High Row fell into this category as we regarded it as so enjoyable, so unique and so symbolic of vintage Darlington that we miss it, but that is just our opinion and others are perfectly entitled to have theirs as this town is here for the benefit of the entire population and not just us. More recent achievements have

Major
architects of
Darlington
and us -
*a personal
view*

been the elegant Art Decor Binns store which although it replaced some old and quaint shops on the corner of High Row and Blackwellgate did it with such style and was such a statement of its era that the loss of those must be forgiven and justified. We can only imagine what a stir it must have caused when it was first built as it would have been the very last word in modern design at that time. Change even to bricks and mortar is inevitable in the end but if important constructions are to be demolished the architecture which replaces them should be exciting, stimulating, stylish and useful but so often the more mundane but cost effective option has to be taken, which seems a shame and sometimes diminishes a locality. We are lucky to have some really excellent new developments here in our town and some of those have only recently been completed in our present time such as those in the Education Village designed by gifted architects at the highly rated company Ryder HKS, or are about to the constructed such as the Oval Centre which, whatever worries one has of what the eventual outcome of the commercial impact of it will have on the town, will certainly have its exterior designed in an impressive and streamlined ultra-modern manner which we think is preferable to it trying to resemble mock Victoriana which could have looked false and a bit like a theme park. I believe the interior will be mock Victorian but of a very high standard and may, given the modern exterior be a pleasant suprise for the people who will use it, but we will have to wait and see as at the time of writing this is all in the future. As we said there have been other buildings which have regretfully been lost to us for various reasons over the years, but some are still recognisable if you look just above the inevitable ground floor corporate facades of the shops and businesses in the town centre (as a young lady named Carys Raper reminded us to do during the course of the survey we did which was mentioned at the beginning of this book), and discover what remains of original buildings which provoke thoughts of past glories, much in the same way as we think that one now needs to look just outside the centre of town to discover the original Darlington.

Beryl Hankin and Colin Harrison.

Snippet

It is believed that one of G.G. Hoskins first commissions was to build no 15 and 16 Westbrook Villas in 1846. These houses and many others in Westbrook Villas are still occupied by proud owners and are still wonderful and inspire the residents enough to have their own association with a site on the internet. Our friends Billy and Betty Inns used to live in Westbrook Villas. Betty was even inspired to write a story about their house when they had to leave to move into a bungalow due to her husband Billy's poor health.

The heartland

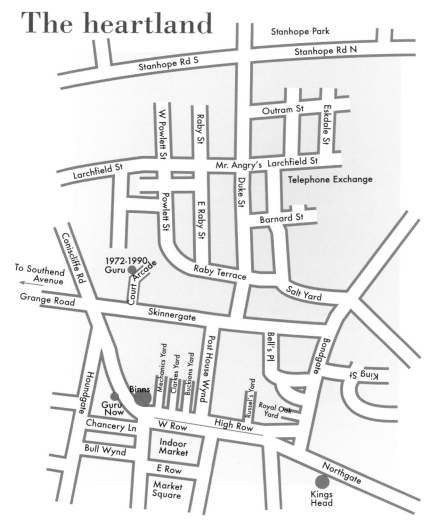

**This is a map of old High Row Darlington's traditional heart,
the yards which are its many arteries (and surrounding areas).**
(included in order to make the locations of some of our stories a bit
clearer for those who don't live here)

Heart Transplant

Where have all the grocers gone
With smells of fresh ground coffee
Where have all the hammers gone
That broke up trays of toffee

Where are all the errand boys
Who wore their cycle clips
Those savoury ducks and saveloys
And scraps with fish and chips

Where have all the rabbits gone
Pigs trotters and cows heels
Where have nuns in habits gone
And cars that had three wheels

Where have all the bobbies gone
With leather gloves and capes
Of men's outfitters there are none
Where from their necks hung tapes

Where have all the hatters gone
The milliners and drapers
Where have all the newsboys gone
Who shouted 'evening papers'

Where's the Northern Despatch
gone
We called 'The Sporting Pink'
Why does Joseph Pease look glum
Whatever must he think?

Where's Victoriana gone
Of which High Row was part
It's undergone the surgery
That gives a town new heart

The old yards are the arteries
To remind us of the blues
The happiest of memories
Are the ones we pick and choose.

Harry Cadman.

Darlington's railway heritage

What an incredible achievement it is for this town have been the 'home' of the Railways. Thanks to Darlington Quaker money provided by the Pease family Robert Stephenson and Company built Locomotion No 1. This was the first ever passenger pulling engine in history and can still be seen at our Railway Museum in North Road. The world's first passenger railway was The Darlington to Stockton line inaugurated in 1825. The local Pease and Stephenson families (and of course great engineers like Timothy Hackworth) were all involved in the experimentation and trials leading up to this momentous venture which began initially out of a need to solve the problem of transporting coal, and subsequently ended up carrying fare paying people. They say 'necessity is the mother of invention' well it certainly was here in this case, and what a world encompassing invention the railways turned out to be. When our market place and Skinnergate underwent refurbishment in the 1990's we thought it was nice to see Railway references in abundance such as tracks in the ground, wheels on town centre seating and sturdy cast iron direction signs topped off with tiny trains. We now also have a train weathervane on top of our town clock too, and of course we have a modern brick train on the outskirts of town. This railway heritage of ours is something to be very proud of as it did radically change the world, and it all began here. This short synopsis of that marvellous feat of engineering has been an extreme simplification of all the skill, inventiveness and rivalry that was involved at the time when the railways emerged as it would have taken volumes to do the subject real justice. The more information one absorbs in relation to rail engineering and planning, the more it becomes apparent that there is a staggering amount more to be discovered.

Ray Hankin.

Postcard from Darlington

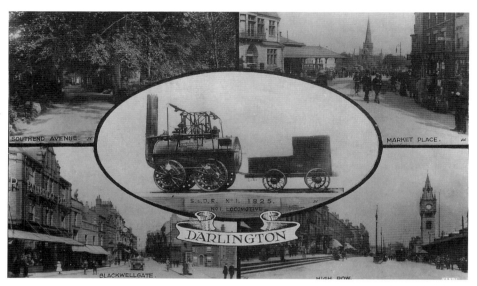

Picture postcard supplied by Bridget Emmerson from her collection of Prudhoes postcards

Drawing by Jean Kirkland

The day football ruled on High Row!

'Ere we go, 'ere we go High Row

Football both amateur and professional has been very important to Darlington since as far back as the1800's. Darlington Football Club has one of the most fascinating histories of all the clubs around. In recent years we have seen many changes to the 'Quakers' as they are known. One of the most impressive and controversial is the building of the fantastic modern 25,000 seater stadium and the circumstances surrounding it. True supporters with a passion for their club will follow that club whatever happens and will turn out to cheer them on when they succeed. This is evident in this photograph taken by Mr John Patrick Walsh, who was present when on the 1st of June 1985 Darlington football team made a triumphant ride down the old High Row in an open topped bus to celebrate their promotion to the (then) third division. They were to stay there for two years and then dropped down again. At the end of the 88/89 season the club was relegated to the Conference league but legendary manager Brian Little took them back up again at the first time of asking. The club is in league two at the time of writing this and I'm sure we all wish Darlington F C loads of luck in the season ahead.

Tony Smith.

Photograph supplied by Mr. John Patrick Walsh

(In the piece which follows in spite of being occupied with her own task of getting home from town in the midst of a post match crush, the lady who penned it was obviously in touch with all the details of what was going on around her and recognised a sense of romance in the scene which she was part of. Other less aware beings may have just regarded it simply as a nuisance and never thought of it again. People like Pauline are the lucky ones in life as even whilst being practical and realistic they can see beyond the obvious and enjoy the spirit and colour within a situation and get the most out of things.

Sporting Pink

It was like a Lowery painting!

A haze of pink and brown at 5pm on a Saturday afternoon – men in macs and trilbys carrying the 'pink' newspaper, rushing for their buses after a football match at Feethams had finished. Not a good time to return home after shopping. All the buses were full to standing – men going home to check their 'scores', hoping Littlewoods Pools had been good to them (top prize £1,000!!). The 'pink' was the sports newspaper only printed on a Saturday – a bright pink at that. The High Row would be full, the bus stands overflowing and I would be wishing I'd gone home at 4pm.

Pauline Rees.

Photograph supplied by Mr. John Patrick Walsh

'Before the Storm'

Original Painting by Tony Hughes

Message from the artist...

"Just a quick note to say the picture is called "Before the Storm" which I suppose seems a little bit appropriate bearing in mind the changes.

It was painted early one Sunday morning sitting in Boyes doorway about 30 years ago. The weather was beautiful to start with and changed so many times it became impossible to carry on painting so it was 'tidied up' at home over quite a number of years. When it was really overcast the brightest things to see were the road traffic signs."

Memories of High Row

High Row, Darlington in my teens

By a Darlington resident, now a pensioner

It was a carousel as we walked round and round, hearts racing, hearts pounding and hearts hoping. Hoping to meet the boy of our dreams. And if we did, nothing ever happened except for a rather shy conversation occurring with lots of laughter, nervous laughter, for this was the innocent generation where dreams were dreams and our young lives depended on them. We, the post war youth had little else.

Except perhaps, the choice of jobs when we left school. Peases Mill Factory, Patons and Baldwins, shop assistants, or if you had risen to shorthand and typing classes perhaps you would reach the dizzy heights of becoming a secretary!

But none of it mattered, if you were seventeen and earned thirty shillings a week, as I did, and could afford an agonizing pair of high heels, to walk in after tea, along the High Row, past Binns and Grisedales (ladies outfitters), past Dressers (the stationers) and Lucks, that latter whose annual sale always provided my gown or posh dress for the major highlights of the year as a young girl. What a shop it was, to be sure. Full of buttons and ribbons and up the winding staircase the fabulous hats and dresses, the latter which must have been samples for they were most unusual. I bought a satin dress there. A tight fitting beauty that showed off my young figure, that went in at all the right places, then… I bought a balloon dress there, billowing out from the waist and tight around the calves, so I could only walk tiny steps and these were two of my most outstanding gowns for The Civic Theatre or the Press Ball, which were always held in Gladstone Street, in the Baths Hall. Young men, uncomfortable in dinner suits with bow ties danced round the floor with you, and later walked you home in a polite manner, perhaps kissing you on the cheek, before a parent would appear (usually your father), telling you it was time you were in the house. You whispered 'See you on the High Row, tomorrow evening' and you knew he would be there.

And so you donned the high heels once more ('surely they will be worn in by now') and the dirndl skirt with layers and layers of lacy petticoats, which was called 'the new look' and so the parade began again for dozens of local youngsters. We met the same people over and over again, as we circulated in this main centre of the town. It was a meeting place, a show off area, a place to be seen and a rendezvous for the young people of Darlington, who would take in the strong ground coffee smells from Fox's café and the pungent aromas of assorted fresh fish from Aitkins the fishmongers. People then knew how to behave and would never vandalise the town they loved and were proud to live in. Others who remember these days, as I do, will now be in their seventies. Glorious days, gorgeous memories, a classy High Row, but now, alas, gone forever….

Anonymous.

(This lady did not supply a name or an address but at least we can thank her here for her wonderful addition to this book).

High Row heydays

Born in 1921 at my grandparent's home near Gladstone Street, my earliest memories of High Row were as a very young child being taken to town on Saturday nights to see all the shops lit up and decorated for Christmas. Like all children, I recall being entranced at the scene; the High Row was fairyland.

All the shops were open and trading until 9 or 10pm. The Salvation Army Band would be playing to a host of onlookers at the foot of Pease's monument until prompt at 9 o'clock when it (and the crowd) would form up to march off to the Citadel.

This was the time to buy fruit, meat and vegetables, for without refrigeration or storage everything had to be sold or thrown away. Sunday dinner for the whole family could be bought for a few coppers all around High Row.

Sunday nights were different. Town shops, although closed, left their windows lit until 7 or 8pm, and the High row became the parade of the town's teenagers – lads and lasses who, split into two equal halves and walked round and round – along High Row, up Blackwellgate, along the length of Skinnergate, down Bondgate and back along the Row again. Post House Wynd was changeover point where one could reverse direction and thus meet all the lads and lasses who had previously been going the same way as you. Many Darlington families owe their origins to the High Row perambulation for there were many dark Yards and doorways. There was never any hint of disorder or bad language. There was drama too, usually on market day (Monday) when a young bullock or heifer would escape its handlers at the cattle market to career across town and market place, to end up in one of the pubs or in one of the High Row shops causing havoc among shoppers and trades people alike until being finally tethered to the High Row railings.

One personal memory I recall was utter ruination of my family's Christmas when I must have dropped four one pound notes outside a bank on High Row, my weekly wage was four pounds and ten shillings, not realising until I arrived home. By this time the banks were closed for the festive period.

Watercolour Painting by Peter Vart

The High Row will always be noted for the huge fire of 1925, which destroyed the entire store of H Binns & Son drapers' outfitters. At the time it consisted of several shops joined to each other on various levels, which made for a spectacular blaze. The present building was built and opened in 1927. Considering its age it is a fine building, which does not look out of place even now. Another feature was the huge Gilt Top Hat. This adorned the premises of a gents outfitters, of much distinction. Their gilded Top Hat stood out on High Row for all to see.

One was always conscious while shopping on High Row for mundane items like butter or eggs at "Home & Colonial" or a few lamb chops at Peacocks Butchers, that a few yards away on the other side of the railings and said to be valuable (but now gone) pink marble steps, there passed one of the great arteries of Britain – the Great North Road to Scotland complete with a policeman resplendent in white armlets, holding the nation's traffic up while Darlingtonians made their way from Binns to the indoor market. Where else could such a phenomenon be seen? As a vantage point to see the world it remained unsurpassed, as there was no ring road or roundabout on the old A1. Any elder with time on his hands could sit on the High Row and see sights like the 1st Battalion Durham Light Infantry marching at a rate of knots through Darlington on a busy Saturday with drums beating, bayonets fixed and colours flying, as was their right. A bronze propeller on a lorry destined for some big ship building at Camel Lairds, a huge 100ft long 10ft diameter catalyst cracking column on a Pickfords low loader wending its way to the South round Binns corner in the general direction of Fawley refinery, or the two mile long railwaymen's carnival processions with dozens and dozens of decorated flats and four or five bands, all to raise funds to build the town's Memorial Hospital in the late thirties.

Look in any old photographs and you will see how people shopped in days gone by. Few got wet in rainy weather because all the shops had sunblinds and canopies to protect their goods and customers. There were colourful awnings and bead curtains to keep out the flies. Chewing gum had yet to cross the Atlantic, but there were plenty of fag ends and matches.

If only Pease could tell of all he has watched as he looks out from Prospect Place along High Row, past Backhouses Bank (later Barclays) and the town clock to the old town hall, what would we learn?

In conclusion, a personal impression is that like the bombed-out Birmingham New Street Station footbridge over the platforms (if one stayed there one would eventually see everyone in the world one had ever met), to stand in similar fashion on the High Row one would soon see everyone known to you in this town.

One hopes that its new image will be equally as rewarding.

Bill Lawson.

High Row 'water feature'

High Row had a central water feature at the foot of Post House Wynd, which was tolerated by some and hated by many. It was of course, the Gents washroom and toilet.

Accessed by two gated stone stairways it was a seasonal hazard, freezing and treacherous in winter and stinking to high heaven in summer, despite all the hosing and cleaning possible.

It was there for much of the 20th Century, and was a part of the High Row's history. I wonder how many of the regiments that have marched past saluting dignitaries realise they were unwittingly saluting a gents toilet?

The "old" water feature though less palatable than the current water feature was perhaps more functional. At least the old water feature added "atmosphere" to a very busy street!

Bill Lawson.

We sourced this nice Civic photo from the Centre for Local Studies in Darlington Public Library

Snippets

My favourite memory of High Row was the baby shop Phillips which was on the Bondgate side of Luck's. I used to be fascinated by all the little ladybirds in the window. They were magnetised and used to seem to run about. I also liked the old fashioned chemist Hodgson's where they sold things like turtle oil cream which was in a container shaped like a turtle, and hand cream in a plastic bottle that resembled a hand.
Lorraine Jackson.

My memory of the High Row is from a long time ago, but I remember it clearly. I was two years old; my mother was wheeling me in my pushchair up the High Row steps. I looked up and there above Binns was a large silver cylindrical object in the sky, which I later found out, had been an airship.
Joan M Armes.

My fondest memories of the High Row are the shops which have either moved or have closed. They included grocers, haberdashers, bakers and other shops which always had their awnings out on both sunny and wet days. On market days you could not move. People used to stand on the steps talking, and it was a meeting place for all. Darlington had on its lovely High Row something unique which other towns did not have and nobody seems to want to mention, which was the gentleman's toilets situated underground almost opposite Post House Wynd. Any old Darlingtonian would tell you they were a godsend in times of need. They blended in with the rest of the High Row with the marble pillars and iron railings, which stretched from one end to the other. High Row was also renowned as a meeting place to celebrate New Year.
Mr S Summers.

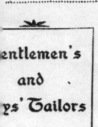

Bought of *Atkinson & Co*

School Outfitters.

Hatters, Hosiers, and Shirt Makers.

5% CHARGED ON OVERDUE ACCOUNTS.

Look for ye Sign
of ye Hat.

Atkinson & Co

I was born in 1915. My parents both had family shops on High Row. My mother's family were Stephenson Bros, number 18, now a shoe shop and my father's shop was Atkinsons & Co, number 24, now an opticians. They were all gentlemans outfitters, hatters and tailors. My great grandfather was Titus Atkinson and my grandfather and father were John and Arthur.

Mother was a waistcoat hand and worked with Mary Brown in her grandfather's shop before she married my father

Atkinson & Co were high class outfitters and hatters for gentlemen and boys, providing school outfits for boys private schools and also bespoke tailoring including hunting regalia. They also repaired silk hats and altered clothing.

Number 24 is best remembered as the shop on the High Row with the hat sign hanging outside, this was sketched by Fothergill.

I can always remember the hat sign hanging outside our shop. My twin sisters and I only rarely visited the outfitters as children walking down past Sydney Woods in Blackwellgate round Binns corner, looking at the diamond rings in Harrisons the jewellers.

The hat sign was metal and was regularly sent away to be re-covered in gold leaf. During the last war it had to be painted grey in case it glittered as a target for the enemy. The gold leaf had preserved it and not long after the war it fell into disrepair.

Number 24 was the only shop on the High Row with a rear entrance in Talbot's yard off Post House Wynd. There was a cottage at the back of the shop with

The boxing ring in the picture was behind Atkinson's shop in the 1920's. Joan Wright's father Arthur Ainsworth Atkinson is in the picture and he featured in many amateur bouts and even was host to Bombardier Billy Wells from London's East End who was the famous heavyweight champion boxer who won the Lonsdale Belt back in 1911 and later became the "gong man" - the figure striking the gong in the introduction to J. Arthur Rank films. As well as calling in for a friendly sparring session from time to time Bombardier Wells was also a customer of Atkinson's

stabling for four horses and my father Arthur, an amateur boxer, had a indoor boxing ring at the back of the shop where the Vanes, Edens and Bradfords used to practice.

When I was sixteen I left the High School to work in the shop for my father. Working in the shop were Mr Pearson, Nancy Johnson and myself. We were open from 9am until 6pm, closed on Wednesday afternoons, but opened until 8 o'clock every Friday and 9 o'clock every Saturday. The High Row on Saturdays was always busy. We had an hour and a quarter for lunch and thirty minutes tea break, which was staggered. The shop did not close. Everyone biked or walked home there was no eating outside in town in those days.

Customers paid by cash, all the bills were hand written, some had accounts which were always paid promptly. Goods purchased were not carried home by the customers but were delivered to your home by the errand boy on his bike, boxed or wrapped in brown paper.

Some customers such as Lascelles and Lungley, who became governors of Hong Kong and Sarawak, still ordered from Atkinsons such things as umbrellas, silk hats, white shirts and evening suits which were sent out to them by train and boat. The bills were settled two or three years later when they returned.

I was exempted from war service because we did military tailoring for officers. Clothing coupons were used during and after the war years.

It is the shops like Luck's, Liptons and Saxone that are best remembered on High Row but above the shops were other floors for architects, solicitors, stocks and shares bankers. Pritchards, Clayton and Dedes, Fry and Co and Captain Du Leather worked above us.

In latter years we outfitted Darlington Girls High School and provided the Ladies Training College with blazers. Miss Walker was the head of the Training College, now the Arts Centre, and insisted that only a lady measured the girls and my mother had to do this.

The goods we sold were quality, silk hats were a guinea and suits were five guineas. The bespoke suits were made in Leeds by the amazing Jewish tailors Keith Joseph's. The shop display was set out by us with hats, socks, pyjamas and underclothes with the prices only shown for the less expensive goods.

The Darlington Railway Carnival took place in August attended by the Mayor and Corporation. Our shop had the best position looking down Tubwell Row. We decorated the balconies in red, white and blue and sat there to watch. It raised money to build the Memorial Hospital. All shops on High Row paid one penny a week towards this and the money was collected by Stewart Reed.

The High Row has always been very busy on Saturday mornings. At Christmas the shops stayed open until midnight on Christmas Eve lit by gaslight, and we did get late customers.

The shopkeepers always kept the pavements swept and took pride in the frontage, washing and polishing the doors and handles.

My family owned Atkinsons High Row shop for 156 years until it was sold in 1972. The original deeds show a house, stables and orchard but it was rebuilt into a shop by my great grandfather Titus. We never lived on High Row.

Joan Wright.

Joan Wright and her twin sisters

P.S.

Another interesting snippet about Atkinson's wonderful shop is that Arthur Ainsworth Atkinson the proprietor always took his dogs to work with him, and every day as soon as one of those dogs (a beautiful black Labrador) heard the five o'clock buzzer go at North Road Railway shops (which was audible on High Row in those days), this dog would get up and head off for home either on its own or with one of Atkinson's errand boys running behind to make sure it got there safely.

When I was a Kid

I remember High Row when I was a kid,
I often look back on some of the things that I did.
It was back in the early seventies,
that was a time like heaven to me.

Most of the things I did often make me laugh,
and I would often venture into the Golden Egg café,
I would spend most of my days roaming up and down,
just hanging about in the town.

There was Boots, Dressers and Binns,
some of the stores I would often go in,
but now that times have changed and I have grown,
I'll never forget my childhood memories
Of times along High Row.

© Michael Muszynski.

Freedom

In the late 60's after work when I was an apprentice at Brown's Sawmills my mates and I use to ride down to High Row on our motorcycles and park up and just hang about with the bikes all in a row. I think a lot of it was just showing off. After a while we would bump start the bikes, jump on the seat and belt down High Row in first gear. It really sounded good. Turn right and down Tubwell Row and straight up Yarm Road. No lights and no roundabouts then, it was just great!

The really best bit about the whole thing is that I met my wife there on High Row, and here we are thirty five years later still involved with classic motorcycles and still going strong. Those times were the best ever and we have wonderful memories. The next generation will never know how it was.

Mr and Mrs P R Lee.

Tales of High Row

Being in my teens in the mid forties the High Row at night was strictly taboo for me, considered by the older generation as a place of disrepute. Not exactly a red light district you understand, but a place where no respectable lass would frequent. For this reason on our visits to the three picture houses in that area, myself and four sisters had to make a detour, and it would have been God help us had we disobeyed mum's express orders.

I can't remember the name of the shoe shop at the far end, it could have been Timpsons, but I still remember the beautiful shoes mum bought me for my sixth birthday from there. They were red patent leather and I loved them. I danced along High Row wearing them like Dorothy on the 'Yellow Brick Road'.

Dresser's was always a magical place to window gaze, as it was packed with lovely china and unusual ornaments. Hodgsons the old fashioned chemist's shop was the last place in town to stock 'infant preservative' a cure for all babies ills, and much prized by mothers back then.

My father came into possession of a very ancient five pound note with the name 'Backhouses Bank, High Row' on it. I showed it to someone in the museum who sent me to Barclays Bank, and

I was told that the present Barclays was on the same site as the bank known once as Backhouses Bank and they still had a few of these old fivers in their vaults. After reading up on this prominent Darlington family in the library, I discovered they were involved with the Pease family, through marriage and business.

Our largest department store Binns has always been a magnet for shoppers and is still there and I hope going strong.

One very sad memory of the High Row for me happened on one Christmas Eve. It was very cold and snowing heavily. I saw a familiar figure with a bushy red and grey beard and wearing a duffle coat coming towards me. I knew him to be homeless as I had seen him many times before. He was a proud man who never begged or even spoke to anyone, just silently accepting whatever money you pressed into his hand. I remember being surprised by the warmth of his hand on such a cold day. The day after Boxing Day I read in the 'Echo' that a man had been found dead on Christmas day in the doorway of Saxone. He had died from the bitter cold, and the police were appealing for relatives or anyone who knew his name to come forward but no one did. People just called him 'the old man', although I guess he was less than fifty years old. He was buried without a name: some mother's son ...so sad.

High Row has seen it all. The Old High Row was different from any other town, it set us apart from the ordinary, and it had a special character unlike most of these newly developed town centres that have a feeling of ordinariness about them. I imagine few of my generation will welcome the loss of this unique place, but then what do I know?

Mary Burnside.

Memories of High Row in days gone by

I will start my memories with New Years Eve.

People young and old would congregate on High Row to see the old year go out and the new year come in. What a happy atmosphere it was.

High Row was a good walking place on a Sunday afternoon for all. It was nothing for a young lady to walk along and drop a lovely white handkerchief in the hope of a young man picking it up and taking it to her. A love match was often made on High Row.

In day's gone by ladies stockings had a black seam down the back of the leg. Young ladies loved them and when out walking they would often look back over their shoulder to see if the seam was straight, this was often done on High Row, another way to attract a young man. Every thing was done in good fun.

One of my memories of High Row was going with my late husband to Binns Café for a cup of tea and a cream scone, we never stopped talking to each other, they were happy days with lots of memories.

High Row was one of the ideal places for people to meet. It was good for courting couples because they could shelter in the doorways. High Row had a lot of advantages for people and in this respect still has.

Shops would close half a day on a Wednesday and all day on a Sunday, but it was always lovely to walk along High Row to see the well dressed shop windows.

Luck's the Drapers was a wonderful shop where one could buy anything from a packet of pins upwards, I loved to go shopping in that shop.

I loved Dressers the Stationers, that shop had a lot of memories for me, especially when I look at the presents that I have been given over the years bought there.

I will always have memories of the man selling the Evening Despatch on High Row in all weathers I was sorry for him. In later years a lady took over from him, she had her own seat, she sat facing Post House Wynd. She was selling papers there until the Evening Despatch closed down.

The jewellery shop that was on the corner of High Row and Post House Wynd was where my son, 15 years of age bought me a pair of dropped ear rings. That was 50 years ago, and I still have them and my memories.

I will finish my memories in the month of December when High Row would be all dressed up with Christmas decorations, a lovely large tree, lights, and all the shops looking like Christmas with reindeers in the windows of Dressers Shop.

Betty Inns.

On Old High Row

Leaning on the railings
Up on old High Row
You could watch the hustle bustle
And the buses come and go

The benches often brimming
It really was a treat
To find a place not taken
And have yourself a seat

Jostling for their places
Were shoppers all aglow
With smiles and friendly faces
Up on old High Row

Who shuffled into shops
And scurried into inns
And hurried to the market hall
For cabbages and tins

You never could be lonely
As you'd spot someone you know
And chat away for ages
Up on old High Row

If the Richmond bus was late
Then Mrs Wright's not stopping
She's only half an hour, you know
To finish off her shopping.

And there goes Mrs Turner
With children all in tow
And she clips their ears quite soundly
As they walk along High Row

And What about the workers
Who scurry for their lunch
And walk along whilst chewing
And talking in a bunch

You could watch the world revolving
And traffic on the go
As you leaned upon the railings
Up on old High Row.

Grace Gant.

Salvation row!

Many have had cause to be grateful for the shelter and assistance afforded by the 'army' and many more have warmed to the sight of their 'soldiers' collecting in even the most rowdy pubs in the town and to the sound of the rousing music from their band.

Hymns of comfort

My earliest memory of High Row was in wartime. Having launched myself into the big wide world, I began my first job at Darlington Memorial Hospital. I was the first medical secretary to be employed there, and the only one for the first three years'.

I used to travel to Darlington by bus from Wensleydale on Sunday evenings to be greeted by the Salvation Army playing my favourite hymns on High Row. At first I felt rather homesick having just left home and had fond memories of singing hymns round the piano on Sunday evenings.

Whenever I hear the band now I think of those very happy years spent in Darlington and of course High Row.

Elma Banks (nee Chapman).

Fond memories

During the Second World War I was a member of the Salvation Army junior band and I am sure many people will remember the senior band and the songsters on the High Row on a Sunday evening giving lots of pleasure to the people there.

There was a Company Sergeant Major called Mr Ward who used to shout for 'a penny on the drum'. What happened was that the base drum was laid flat on the ground and people were asked to throw coins onto the drum. The money was collected and went to help people who were not so well off.

My Uncle Harold Pretty was the junior band master and I played the trombone and was involved in playing music to the crowds who used to come to High Row on Sunday evenings. What a pity things have changed for they were good times then on the High Row.

All my sincere best wishes to the Darlington people and the High Row.

Wilf Pretty.

Joyful sound

My memory of the High Row is happy Sunday nights
We stood strong together singing and felt things would be all right
Though it was many years ago the memory will never fade
As a family we stood with the Salvation Army,
We all talked and sang and we prayed.
The band was one to be proud of, the songsters a joy to hear
The people around were pleased to join in,
Tom Raines voice could be heard loud and clear,
At that time there was conflict in the world
People needed that joyful sound
It raised their spirits gave them hope
You could see as you looked around
There were some who found their hearts were lighter
As they joined in the singing and prayer
Later they followed us back to the Citadel
Lasting friendships were also made there
It was a wonderful feeling to be part of that crowd
Do you think it could happen again
Will we hear once again that band on High Row
Or will they be put off by the rain!

MH (Mrs M. Hudson).

The ladies in the picture are
Mrs M. Hudson's mother and a friend
dressed in their Salvation Army uniforms

There are many and varied comments about the Salvation Army. I remember one night a young man spoke to my mother and asked, "do you save fallen women?", "Yes" said mum. "Will you save the next one for me then?", replied the young man.

M.H.

Junior band

Salvation Army junior band (1943) Picture supplied by Wilf and Celia Pretty.
Members of the band. Top row 1st left - Tom Raine. Boy with cornet is Mr and Mrs Pender's son who rose to be Commissioner. Middle row 3rd from left - Wilf Pretty. Centre with drum is Mr Pretty's uncle Harold the junior band master. To the left of him is Adjadent Pender and to the right of him is Mrs Pender. 1st boy on the second from the bottom row is James Dauber and I'm sure many more people reading this will recognise relatives.

Mr. Pretty who supplied the band picture was once part of a well known variety act called Wilf and Ted Cousins (Wilf and Ted really were cousins hence the stage name). They were billed as "the boys that will impress you" and entertained by performing comedy, harmony, singing and impressions.

This photo is of Tom Raine, a wonderful singer and stalwart member of the Salvation Army who was loved and respected by all

Me and my mate Marlene

After school back in 196?? (not saying) everybody used to head for the High Row, as it was where 'everybody' used to meet, and this was where I used to meet my mate Marlene. We used to stand about looking cool, eyeing up all the posh boys from the Grammar School.

One Sunday afternoon me and Marlene were sitting in our usual pose (cross legged) on High Row. As we watched the Salvation Army band playing a few hymns we decided to sing along with them. We were quickly spotted (sadly not by Simon Cowell), by the Sali Army band master who asked us if we would like to march back to the Citadel with the band. So me and my mate Marlene, in true groupie style up for anything, followed on doing our impersonations of George Harrison's Hare Krishna. On arrival at the Citadel we were asked to stand in front of the congregation with our newly acquired tambourines and join in with two verses of 'Onward Christian Soldiers' (eat your heart out Mary Hopkins). Sadly however they were not able to save our souls, but it made for a nice change on a Sunday afternoon.

The High Row later became our regular meeting place for trips to Teesside Airport disco, and then the obligatory hitch hike to Kirk Levington Country Club where we used to sing along with Mike Coles and Little Jo', mainly about her baseball boots! We were now officially fully fledged hippies (peace man or should I say Marlene?).

High Row was also the venue for my big brother (well we're both the same size actually), Iain (alias Pricie). He used to meet his mate George Palmer (alias Jungle) on the High Row with the rest of his mates on a Friday night, usually after the pubs fell out, mainly from the (then named) County (gas lamp room), and I remember there always seemed to be a fight, but then they weren't hippies like me and my mate Marlene, they were big bad bikers! Which was pretty cool for me and Marlene as everbyody knew that my big brother was a big bad biker too so we were alright.

A short (but true) story by Suzanne Binks (nee Bright).

Suzanne Bright and Marlene Mangle

Time traveller on High Row

On the 23rd of December 1943 a time traveller was born in Orchard Road, Darlington, covered in a white powder which turned out to consist of all that was left of the massive number of Rennie tablets her mam had taken to try and ease the heartburn which this eight pounds baby girl had caused her to suffer during her pregnancy.

Photo of the time traveller taken in Binns in 1946 (aged three)

My mam often used to tell me that on the first market day in Darlington after my birth that she was well enough to do so, she and my handsome dad on leave from the army, took a stroll down town and proudly pushed me in my pram along the full stretch of High Row, as that was the place to go and be seen by a good crowd of people. This was the first of many such visits, usually with my mam and nana, as my dad (Rupert) had gone back to his regiment, to buy essentials like liberty bodices for me from 'the ladybird shop' as they referred to it, which was one of the many magical retailers along that wonderful row of businesses. I don't know it by name but one shop had a big wooden carved Indian standing outside its door, and delicious aromas of spices and coffee drifted out to tempt people inside as they stood there admiring him.

1949. Aunty Maureen and Uncle Roland came through from Teesside to give me a rare Christmas treat of an outing to Binns (which was regarded as the swankiest department store around), to see Father Christmas. I remember as we approached this marvellous place I searched the winter sky for a sight of Santa and his reindeer flying across far above High Row on their way to the roof of Binns. I was a bit worried when I didn't see them, but hoped it was because they were there already, and of course they were, and I was just so overwhelmed and excited that when I was finally accompanied into Santa's Grotto, saw shadows of the reindeer on the walls and was handed a present by the great man, I couldn't even speak.

Whenever we went to town from that day on I always asked to be taken to look into Binns windows.

1959. I left school aged fifteen and straight away got a job at Prudhoes the stationers in Bondgate, and enrolled in a night school art class at Darlington's Northgate College and met a boy called Ray there, who although I didn't know it at the time was to become my future husband. Ray plucked up courage one night after class to ask me out for a drink, which was sort of our first date. I accepted nervously and he walked me up from Northgate, along High Row (where we shared our first kiss, well more a swift peck on the cheek, just as we passed the end of Post House Wynd), to the Imperial cocktail bar. Going into a smart bar with a young man seemed to me to be a very daring and grown up thing to do, that was until he asked me what I'd like to drink. He didn't know I was only fifteen as I looked more like nineteen (which was his age), with my backcombed beehive hairstyle (complete with Helen Shapiro style cheek curls), and dressed in my tight white polo neck jumper, black and white checked pencil skirt and high heeled court shoes, and I was too embarrassed to tell him I was too young to be bought alcohol, so I blurted out the name of the only drink I could think of, "gin and orange please". He told me sometime afterwards that he thought I must be very sophisticated. We then went to where he had parked his Rudge motorbike and he offered me a lift home on the pillion of it, to Haughton (where I lived at that time), but having no sense of direction I couldn't tell him the way, which made me feel very silly. Somehow he managed to find it and then rode off, probably thinking I was a bit retarded, back to his parent's home in Bishop Auckland where he lived. My directional dyslexia as I have now christened it, has been a source of amusement to us ever since, and to this day I have difficulty telling left from right. Our teacher at night school was a wonderful gentleman called Arthur Hughes who (amongst other things) was a commercial artist and had The Art Shop and Art Posters (two linked properties side by side) in Northgate, and soon I went to work for him as his studio assistant there. One of my favourite jobs was to be dropped off by car on High Row on a certain day every week by Mr Hughes, with rolls of posters and three big buckets of paste and a brush, and be left there all morning to paste the cinema posters and other adverts we had prepared at Art Posters (which was the commercial art side of his business), on the hoardings which ran all along it at that time.

Ray in 'that black leather bike jacket' (1960)
Beryl sporting her 'Helen Shapiro' style hairdo, at Springfield School

1961. After almost two years with Mr Hughes I reluctantly left to sample the 'glamour' of a well paid (three pounds and ten shillings a week) job in Binns advertising department which was on the top floor of my beloved department store. So now I was working not just on High Row but in Binns. I had arrived…

My favourite season on High Row was late winter, as it meant you came out of work into the busy darkness of early December evenings, lit by the lights from the shop windows and the streetlights,

Ray and Beryl (1962)

to mingle with all the other people who worked in offices and finished at five, going home or doing a last bit of shopping, before they caught their bus or made their way out of town by some other means. I can remember always stopping to gaze in wonder at the fantastic fairy tale town clock, set against the dark sky and the moon, which was usually visible just above its pointed tower. It is a sight I never tire of and have always felt very lucky to have it available to me to lift my spirits in my home town. Best of all was Christmas Eve on High Row as you always got paid on Christmas Eve even if it wasn't quite pay day, and I used to dash straight out of Binns into all the shops along the row searching for presents for my family, and usually ended up feeling very pleased with myself, in the old fashioned chemists shop Hodgson's buying any Coty L'aimant perfume, talc and soap sets, and Old Spice aftershave packs they had left, to give to my family whether they liked them or not.

1962. I reluctantly left Binns to become a GPO telephonist (or 'hello girl' as we were known). The reason for leaving was that as a telephonist I could earn the heady amount of just over six pounds a week, with the chance of overtime and that was just too good a wage to turn down.

Every work morning I would alight from the bus from Haughton at about 8.30am; and pop up onto the High Row to be greeted by a fresh faced young GPO engineer (who worked at the Barnard Street exchange too). He always waited on High Row to meet me, so as to escort me to work, and we never got any closer than that pleasant walk to the telephone exchange to-gether, but it was very nice as he always used to shyly pay me compliments on the way such as "you always look like a cover girl" or "you manage to look like a fashion model day after day". I'm certain I didn't but it was flattering that he thought so, and it used to make me blush.

Anyway I was going out with Ray the boy from Bishop Auckland with the black leather jacket, the quiff and the motor bike, so the telephonist and the telephone engineer were never going to be more than friends. In 1963 Ray and I got married and I changed jobs yet again, but this time for sad reasons which I won't go into here, but it was an interesting if troubled time...

We lived in a flat in Grange Road, so down that road, into Blackwellgate and along High Row was the way to get to the bus stops, the shops, and the van that picked me up for work at my new job at Paton & Baldwins woollen mills every weekday. It was also the route where about that time I sometimes encountered artistes who had appeared the night before at the LaBamba night club,

1969 - Members of Mother's Lament
and the girls
L to R. Kenny, Rita, Doug, Viv, David,
Beryl and Rob
On a trip away in the group's Commer van
(Ray's taking the photo)

which was also in Grange Road (above the Blue Lagoon which was, and still is, one of our favourite places to eat), and some of these performers would stay over at the Imperial Hotel. No I'm not a stalker it was just coincidence, but I must admit I have followed from Grange Road to the corner of High Row all these big names…Tom Jones, Diana Dors, Englebert Humperdink, Marianne Faithful and quite a few more!

It was 1967 when Ray moved from Bishop Auckland College to work at Darlington College of Technology, and started to manage a rock group called Mother's Lament. The favourite meeting place for the lads in the group was The Green Dragon pub in Post House Wynd, so when the band weren't playing somewhere our night life started to usually involve spilling out onto High Row after closing time to say our rowdy farewells to our friends who were catching their last bus home, whilst Ray and I walked towards Coniscliffe Road where we had bought a house. Those were really good times during which I discovered a whole new world of rock, rhythm'n'blues and soul music, and all that went with it. My LP collection suddenly included Otis Reading, Jimi Hendrix, Cream, Led Zeppelin, The Rolling Stones, Jethro Tull, Them, Free, The Kinks and many of the old blues masters, all bought either from Binns or George A Williams record departments. On bank holidays we sometimes took a trip in the group's Commer van with members of Mother's Lament and their girlfriends, down to London to explore amazing places like Soho, Kensington Market and Carnaby Steet when swinging London was at its peak. I remember one night scouring Wardour Street in the hope of finding an underground dive where we might catch a performance by Pink Floyd, and ending up instead seeing Slade (when they still wore braces and bovver boots), at the famous Marquee club. Another time we ventured out to The Railway Hotel in West Hampstead which hosted a rhythm and blues club in its function room known as Klooks Kleek, but we were several years too late to catch The Yardbirds or Ten Years After playing there. We all slept like sardines in sleeping bags in the van, which we parked on a car park in Wright's Lane off Kensington High Street, and the camaraderie was brilliant. On a morning we'd go to the public loos near Kensington Town Hall to wash and freshen up, stepping over the rather dubious long haired people who were in there already sitting about on the floor. To me it was all a great adventure, and from one of these trips to London I returned to Darlington with an Afghan coat, probably one of the very first to have been seen as far North as Darlo, and of course where did I go the first time I wore it to show it off? Well High Row of course, and boy did I turn a few heads. I assumed they were all looking at my Afghan admiringly, but they were more likely thinking what the heck is that? These trips to London and my interest in the emergent music scene were such powerful influences on me, and were to be the inspirations behind the shop which I would one day have, Guru Boutique. I had always been addicted to reggae, pop, rock and indeed most exceptional music and musicians (especially my all time hero Paul Robeson), and now in addition I was falling under the spell of the Californian contingent of singers and songwriters (Joni Mitchell, Buffalo Springfield and the like) and this musical discovery was something else again…it was a lifestyle.

Jean, Ray Vincent, Beryl and Dave in London 1967

I'm glad to say I've been adding new music and new experiences to my life ever since, and still am…and as my music collection evolves I hope I do too. I never discard valuable earlier favourites for new tastes, but keep them all, living in harmony in my record collection and in my psyche as an important part of me, as they are all there for different reasons.

It was also about this time that my lovely brave mam Irene who had just been to a hospital appointment on her own, unexpectedly met me from work at the place where I got dropped off every night, and as we slowly walked along High Row to-gether she revealed that the doctor had told her that she had cancer of the womb.

We were both devastated because in addition to all the other things that were going wrong for both of us at this time, this was absolutely the worst news possible as we were so close to each other. I am more than glad to say that after a botched operation and a lot of complications she did eventually make a full recovery…but the day she told me that worrying news was probably the most frightening in my life up to that time.

I liked working at Paton & Baldwins as a telephonist very much, but it was difficult to get there if I missed the van, so after a year or so I applied for and got a job back in town in the advertising department of the Northern Echo. I loved this job even more, as I was fascinated by the work of the journalists and printers and the smell of the newsprint from the big printing presses that rolled there at that time. My mam was getting better by now and almost every lunch time she'd meet me out of work and we'd go along High Row to Binns restaurant for a snack, and she'd often treat me to a present too, even 'though she had very little money. I shouldn't have allowed her to do this, but on one occasion we went into the part of Binns where they had a few racks of vinyl records, and she bought me the LP 'Bridge Over Troubled Water' by Simon and Garfunkel. It cost two pounds, three shillings and sixpence (which was a lot of money in those days), and I thought it was one of the most wonderful things I had ever heard, and still have it to this day as a treasured possession. I then moved on to work in the office of Darlington solicitors Freeman, Daly and

Johnson and following that did a short period as a fundraiser for cancer research. Through all these changes my mam was always there to keep me right and we were always each others best friend. Our next move was to bring us even closer as when I left the job with the cancer charity to become the manageress of a failing leather clothing shop called Skin Trend in Post House Wynd, I gave my mam a part time job there too. We couldn't save this shop as it was already on its way out and we became redundant. Having got a taste for fashion shop work however, we both decided to stay in that particular line of business. It was she and my dad who opened our first attempt at creating a boutique in a lock up shop in North Road called Quaker Girl, but it never really worked as it was too far out of the town centre. Undeterred in 1972, she and I took a tiny unit in Court Arcade and called it Guru. Remembering all the weird and wonderful things I had seen in Kensington Market, we began to sell ethnic clothes and gifts, patchouli oil and joss

1974 - Beryl and her mam Irene in Guru in the very early days

sticks, and became possibly the very first 'hippie shop' in the region. We knew then that we had found what we wanted out of life, which was to work alongside each other amongst friends in our own interesting business in the town centre we were so proud of. The rest is history and Guru is still here thirty five years later, albeit in the changed location of 24 Blackwellgate, just around the corner from High Row. I wish my wonderful mother Irene was still here to share it with our staff of Tony, Colin, Kelly and I, who with Sarah and Kay our current Saturday girls still enjoy the Guru experience to the full. We never took holidays as we couldn't afford to, but nonetheless managed to do most of the things we needed to do, and Mam even held the fort at Guru when Tony persuaded me to take time out to study at York University. During the years we have had Guru I have had many more memorable High Row moments. From 1971 until 1981 I worked several nights a week, as well as doing my full time day job at Guru, as a DJ on a mobile disco owned by Ray called Roadrunner, so for years had not had much opportunity to socialise in town in the evenings. One thing that sticks in my memory is that when we finished work at Guru on an evening, and I had to go straight home to get ready to go and work on the disco, my friend Bridie and my mam (who Bridie used to affectionately call 'Mammy Woodentop'), would head down the High Row for a nice meal of egg, beans and chips at the Golden Egg, and I used to feel jealous as I always really wanted to join them. When we eventually stopped doing the disco I had another stint of going down town, and soon got the hang of it again. My favourite haunts as before, were The Green Dragon (unfortunately I just missed the Vic Reeves years in there), The Old Dun Cow and The Bowes. This meant more late night goodbyes on the High Row as we headed for the taxi's, after stoppy backs in one of these pubs, but I'd better not specify which one for obvious reasons. These late night drinking sessions were best conducted on hot summer nights and involved (in my case), lots of rum'n'cokes, the unique banter and wheelings and dealings of the regulars, and the Juke box playing things like George Michael's exquisitely romantic 'Careless Whisper', Dexy's Midnight Runners energetically belting out 'C'mon Eileen', Springsteen's fabulous classic 'Born to Run' and a track on which the lines 'higher baby' were repeated over and over again until they got right into your head, which a friend just reminded me was called White Lines (don't do it) by Grandmaster Flash and Melle Mel. This was also the time when I bought a dinky little dark purple MG Midget motor car with chrome bumpers, and a soft top which you could fold down in the summer. I loved to drive it along High Row (where there were more people to see it close up), turn into Bondgate, go along Skinnergate, then back down Blackwellgate to cruise High Row once more for luck. What a poser eh? My only excuse is that I was so proud of it that I wanted to take it to the best place in town to show it off. I had to sell my little car in 1990 to help finance Guru's move from Court Arcade to Blackwellgate and haven't owned another vehicle since.

1991 was the year we threw a party in The Quaker Café which is just off High Row inside Mechanics Yard, to celebrate the fact that our shop had survived its first year in our new, and more expensive to run, premises. It was a very nice occasion where we were able to thank all our friends who had helped us, and one of the guests was a young Indian businessman who we bought ethnic clothing from called Jiti Varma, who is still a valued friend and supplier. He arrived at the party and seemed to have a good time, but didn't drink much as he was driving back to Newcastle that night. He stayed until nearly all the guests had left and then totally out of the blue said to me "I hope you don't mind Beryl but as I'm here and my van full of stock is parked just outside on the High Row, perhaps you would like to have a look at the merchandise and buy a few things?" So there Tony and I were at the end of the Guru party at about 1am in the morning, inside Jiti's big white van parked on High Row, happily tired and quite tipsy, raking through rails and boxes of clothes and eventually selecting a sizeable order, due to us both being as I said not entirely sober, and then carrying them over into Guru to be priced and hung up the next morning, after which Jiti kindly drove us both to our respective homes.

1993 was Guru's 21st anniversary, so to commemorate that fact we had a mail order catalogue printed, and we took quite a lot of the photo's for it ourselves on a succession of Sundays, using our friends and customers as models, using the shop as our changing room, and popping out to suitable locations in striking distance of Guru to take the photographs. We found several great spots on High Row to use as backgrounds for our fashion shoots, and we particularly liked to use the big Gothic doorway of Barclays bank as a background, or perch a model on the old railings for a more streetwise shot. I'm sorry but I could go on for ages about my special moments involving High Row, such as the excitement of the Christmas markets, the pleasure it always was to browse in Dressers (especially after my friend Colin pointed out that this established bookshop had been around since the time that Charles Dickens was writing his novels), the fact that whenever I had been away somewhere and got near to Darlington on the journey back the mental

Anth and Alice two of our friends and models posing on the High Row railings for the Guru catalogue (1991)

image of the old High Row which was etched into my consciousness would always pop into my mind as the symbol of home, the way I would always head for that special place both when I was troubled and when I wanted to celebrate…and there is so much more I could say. I think I've said enough now however, to convey just how much it has featured in my particular life. I know it has been just as important to many other people also, as some even lived above the shops in days gone by. One gentleman told me whilst I was doing a recent survey about what people thought of the changes to it, that he was born in a room looking down onto High Row and had many treasured childhood memories of growing up there.

So many terrible things happen in other countries of the world, so many beings have to suffer in ways we can hardly imagine, and many more may have difficult lives right here in this town in their own homes, so perhaps the loss of part of a favourite townscape is not as big a deal as all that in comparison, however for me having the classic, familiar, reliable High Row (the look of which blended so perfectly with the remaining historical buildings around it), as a place of comfort and refuge in Darlington has helped me to hang on to the memory of loved one's lost, and to cope with the knowledge of all the aforementioned troubles in both the more personal and the wider scheme of things. I hoped and believed that the pleasing, comforting, attractively balustraded High Row would long be preserved for the benefit of future generations too. I make no apology for lamenting its passing, and I think I've left no one in any doubt as to how much it has touched on my life and what it has meant to me. The way I am trying to look at it is that the only way to cope with premature loss, whether it is of a special person, a special place or anything of real value, is to remember how fortunate one has been to have known and experienced those people, places or things, and to make sure they are remembered as vividly as possible, and that is the object of this essay. In spite of all I have just said, the truth is that I haven't found my balance again yet after being rocked to the core by all that has happened to my town and (as I consider myself so much a part of Darlington), to me also. I find I am having to start all over again just like I did when I first entered this world, on the complicated task of building my comfort zone, so if I may I'll finish by writing the last paragraph of all this in the third person, just as I began this account of how my love affair with the High Row and the town where I grew up came to be.

On the 6th July 2007 a time traveller feels she has arrived far too soon, at the end of a lifelong journey on the old High Row. She regarded that special place with a passion, and is wrestling with a sense of shocked disbelief as she faces a future devoid of it. She is asking herself if this really is the bold new beginning for our town that some now proclaim will benefit us so much, or rather the huge and tragic mistake that at this moment in time she believes it may be. Whatever the truth of the situation turns out to be, this time traveller will never get over the deep sense of devastation the loss of her spiritual home has caused her to feel. Now she must find the strength of character and ingenuity to cope with her sadness because life goes on, and life amongst true Darlingtonians and our many friends who visit us from far and near, is still vastly preferable to life in so many other locations.

The time traveller in the here and now...

Beryl Hankin.

The Golden Egg

Does anyone else remember The Golden Egg … I think it's the Abbey now? Me and Irene (she'll always be Woodentop to me) spent many a happy tea-time in there after a day in Guru (when it was in the Court Arcade) … we ate very healthily in those days! She was (still is, in spirit) a gorgeous person and I loved being with her. We had many a happy laugh – like the day the waitress took our bus fares from the table 'cos she thought it was a tip!

Bridie.

It happened on High Row

On High Row

He sits on the old stone steps of High Row.
a hot summer's day in town
but she's not there.

He watches a bus rattling up the steep rise from Stone Bridge,
gears grinding, engine rumbling as it reaches the top
and threads its way through the crowds of shoppers
at the corner of Tubwell Row.
All about him people pass by, lost in the Saturday afternoon bustle,
while he sits, alone with this thoughts.
No need to rush.
finally he has the time to spare for life,
but she's still not there.

He looks up at the familiar face of the clock,
'It's not so late' he tells himself
but it's well past two
and she's still not there.
Should he go?
or should he wait a little longer?
She wont be long now,
will she?
His eyes search for her among the hundreds of blurred faces
in the summer heat,
in the packed town,
his town, friendly, familiar, comfortable.
He looks at his watch, feels his heart sink a little bit more.
Seems silly to stay,
she won't be coming now.
Maybe just a few more minutes, just 'till half past.
Can't hurt.

Just a few more minutes........

His thoughts turn inward
as he stares unseeing into the endless crowds of people.
Suddenly he is aware that someone is looking at him,
standing at the bottom of the steps, smiling,
the smile takes on a familiar shape.

"I'm glad you waited".

Ian C Rutland.

55

Spirit of High Row

I came to live just outside Darlington when I was ten years old, and I am now eighty eight. I was head girl at the newly built North Road School for girls. I left when I was fourteen and went as an office junior to the Motor Union Insurance Company at the end of Skinnergate and Blackwellgate, looking down to Darlington Market place. We were joined to the Friends Meeting House, and we had a room adjoining which was occupied by the well-known Quaker Mr J E Hodgkin, who had married Miss Backhouse daughter of the famous banker. When Mr Hodgkin was in residence I acted as his junior as well. In the mornings before we had coffee, I was the messenger, doing various jobs for the firm and staff. When Mr Hodgkin was at home, I often had to go to different banks to pay in cheques. I would go to the Westminster bank at the bottom of Blackwellgate, or sometimes to the National Provincial on the High Row. This bank had a narrow but large tiled entrance hall, with a staircase leading upstairs, where the bank guard Mr. Vickerton had his accommodation. I then had to walk on into the banking hall which was wider and very long. There was an iron grill right along the counter with the cashiers behind. One particular morning when I entered there was only one cashier waiting for a customer – there were two customers arguing who should go first, so the cashier signalled to me to slip my paying in book under the grill – the other customers stopped arguing and turned on me, they were very annoyed. I often visited Barclays Bank. I have never even now, been in such a spacious entrance hall; so wide and high, as if the sun was always shining from above. There was a large round table with chairs around it, as if inviting customers to sit down for a while and there were always a good few magazines waiting for people to read. Years afterwards when I was a widow, I often went in to read the Farmer's Weekly to see if any jobs were available for my farming son.

Elsie Pescod.

Drawing by Hilary Heward
(nee Boddy)

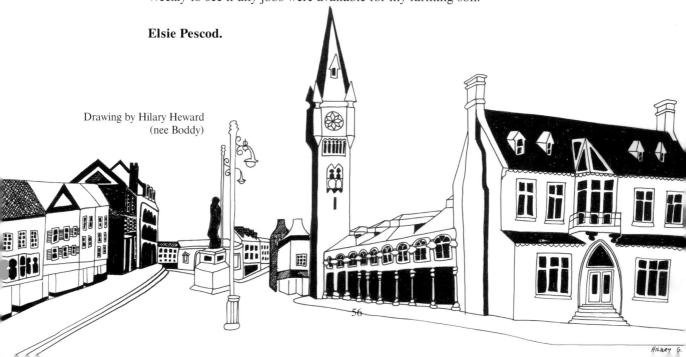

HILARY G.

Memories of Darlington's High Row

I love Darlington with a passion. I was born and bred here and although I left the town for many years following my marriage I returned to my roots nine years ago. Equally I have always loved Darlington's High Row, together with the Market Square and St Cuthbert's Church as these all combined to be the beating heart of the town. Having a 'High Row' built on three levels sets it apart from most other towns.

As a child in the 1930's I remember Atkinsons (with the big hat outside), Lowes, Home and Colonial, Liptons and Luck's (which later became Dressers). If ever I went away on the train as a child, on the return journey I would always stand at the window of the train as we approached Darlington to watch for the first glimpse of 'the blue light' - that meant we were home and I loved to see that light. Probably it was the name "Binns" lit up in blue, I can't remember, but I do remember the excitement it invoked. During the war there was a ceremony held on the centre steps of High Row, attended by the mayor and other dignitaries. I think it was to promote war savings. A representative from each school in the town was chosen to take part, and I was lucky enough to represent Arthur Pease School. I wish I could remember more about that occasion but it was sixty five years ago and all that comes to mind is standing with the other children on a kind of podium and the crowds of people present. It was a big event.

In my teens I sold poppies outside Binns for Remembrance Sunday. There were various sizes of poppies in those days and people who gave a big donation could have quite a splendid poppy almost making a spray for the lapel, and there were decorative ones for cars too.

In the 1930's, 40's and even early 50's the High Row was the shopper's focal point. Everyone "paraded" along the High Row on Saturdays in their smartest clothes and pretty hats. Everyone met everyone there. I looked forward to the day when, if I married and had a baby I would walk along the High Row to show off my baby in a lovely high pram with a fringed canopy (get the picture?) I did indeed marry, have a beautiful baby son, a high black Osnath pram (with a canopy) BUT we moved to Durham when baby was three months old which almost put paid to my dream. I could't let a little thing like that stop me however, so every time I visited Darlington to see my parents or for whatever reason, I came by train and brought the pram in the guard's van so my dream was fulfiled as pram, baby and I bounced proudly along Darlington's main street. My dream came two twofold as I did the same with my second lovely son two years later (they are both in their fifties now).

At general election time it was the High Row that the MP's made for, with crowds gathering round them - I spoke to and shook hands with Michael Heseltine there at one vital election I remember.

So yes, Darlington's High Row with it's quaint yards and it's hustle and bustle played quite a big part in my life and I am sad to have seen it go. As the saying goes "nothing is as constant as change" and change it certainly has.

Sylvia Gargett.

Artists Impression

It is an honour to have in this book the work of one of our finest artists Julian Vasarhelyi, who is an internationally acclaimed stamp designer. Mr Vasarhelyi came here during the political upheavals in his native Hungary many years ago and since then has adopted Darlington as his home and has depicted the town in a series of beautiful drawings.

First Impressions!

I am now a pensioner and not in good health so cannot deal with fuss, but just wanted to say that when my husband and I moved up here from the South fifteen years ago, I didn't know what to expect and was quite upset to be leaving my old home. I felt very homesick and remember my first twenty four hours in Darlington, when after an uncomfortable, unsettled night in our new house, surrounded by half emptied packing cases and cardboard boxes. I had to come down into the town centre to visit Barclays Bank. It all seemed so unfamiliar to me and I parked the car somewhere up Duke Street, and following instructions on the Darlington map I had acquired I made my way into Skinnergate and found Post House Wynd thinking to myself, well this is very nice really, and then I reached the bottom of the Wynd and stepped out onto High Row. It was a sunny day, and it looked so quaint and old worldly. I particularly liked the Urns, and there were flowers everywhere. I stood on the raised pavement for some while, looking out on a wonderful clock tower, and admiring the scene. In that few moments I knew I was going to settle here and that it would soon become my happy new home.

Anon.

Twenty years ago
I came across Darlington High Row
The clock stood tall
Telling time for all.

Beneath lies the indoor market
Shopping in two hours was my target
The Dolphin Centre with games to play
Plenty of hotels for one to stay.

Banks, book shops, bakers three
BHS, M & S, House of Fraser, lots for me
The children found their favourite store
In fact we couldn't ask for more.

My son acted and danced upon the stage,
my daughter became of age,
my husband retired to his allotment,
I found dancing for my enjoyment.

So where oh where
Can there be
a better place
for one to face
the stress of the day
then relax in your own way?

Sandra Moran.

Dressers

On Darlington High Row I bought my first biro

On Darlington High Row
I bought my first biro

In Dressers
God bless us

Where staff were never changed
Or even rearranged

Customer Service
Was invented in here
No noise, no fuss
Just a whisper in the ear

But plenty of noise
Was occurring outside
With wagons and cars
Travelling far and wide

From North to South
To leave or enter
All traffic trundled
Through our town centre

That was the old A1
With its dangers and pollution
And shedding of loads
Because of poor distribution
Many a wagon
Going round Horsemarket bend
Caused a driving career
To come to an end

Winters were magical
With all the shop lights
That seemed to shine brighter
On the very cold nights

Theres's so much to write
But I'll have to stop now
Or else you'll get bored
With when, why and how.

S. Wylie.

So many people apreciated Dressers. It was well established and traditional and the staff always addressed one another formally by their titles of Mr. Mrs or Miss rather than first names and even on the hottest summer day male employees wore collars, ties and jackets. It may have been strict but it was a fabulous shop and is still missed as it sold things you just can't get anywere else, and best of all the staff really cared about their customers.

Below are just two of the many book signings to have taken place in Dressers over the years.

Sept 1994 A young fan gets her book signed at the
launch of "Haghir the Dragon Finder"
by John Dean

Sept 1995 Doreen Dean
author of "Dinosaur Week" signing her book

The town clock

The clock tower above our beloved High Row

For he is Darlington's own Big Ben
He let's you know when it's quarter to ten
He stands amidst our own High Row
And watches the shoppers as they to and fro'

A number of times he's happened to stop
And on heritage days you can walk to the top.

He's overlooked rooftops of many shops close by
Which once upon a time, but now gone like a flash
Were used to freely advertise
Their 'Fish & Chips' or even a 'café'.

And on market days but not recently
A sandwich board man you'd see
Walking up and down the High Row steps
Carrying the words of the Lord at his bequest

The best shop of all was Dressers for me
For my Christmas toys or stationery.

As time ticks on the face of High Row changes
But will always be remembered
As one of many meeting places
Like the market place, Pease's statue or under the clock
Down one of the yards or at the market cross

I'm 'peased' to see you all look up to me
And my colleagues from way back
So speaks the town clock.

Ian Scott.

*Footnote from Beryl - It's nice that Ian
has arranged the lines of his poem to
form steps reminiscent of High Row*

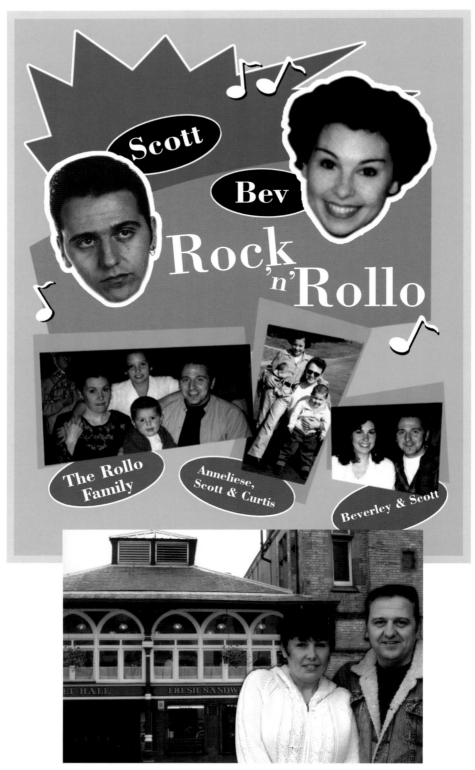

Scott

Bev

Rock 'n' Rollo

The Rollo Family

Anneliese, Scott & Curtis

Beverley & Scott

Scott Rollo and the girl he took to Darlington in his fine poem.
He and his wife Beverley had this picture taken recently near the cafe where they go

62

I took my girl to Darlington

I took my girl to Darlington, not long ago it seems,
The heavens opened up and all the gutters ran like streams,
We walked along High Row, I stopped and kissed her in the rain
And asked her if she'd still be mine when the sun came out again.

As people ran for cover, we held hands and wandered on,
I felt like shouting right out loud and telling everyone,
But the rain washed out the traders, who packed away their wares,
So we headed for the market, to the cafe up the stairs.

I had enough for coffee's and a slice of toast for two,
And we sat beside the window for an hour or a few,
Just watching folk with rain hats and brollies to and fro,
And a couple just as much in love in the bus shelter below.

I took my girl to Darlington but this time it had snowed,
And this girl was my "daddies girl" and all could see it showed,
I took her to see Santa Claus and all the pretty lights,
And right away I knew that this was one of those magical nights.

Music came from everywhere, we danced along High Row,
With tinsel wrapped around our necks and singing as we go,
Then back upstairs to the cafe to sit down before I drop,
While my girl feasts on beans and chips and purple fizzy pop,

I took my boy to Darlington with my girl and their mam,
Though he was only ten months old and had a thing for jam,
He stole the hearts of ladies in the cafe where we go,
And ate ice cream while sitting in his push chair on High Row.

My boy is almost sixteen now, his sister twenty two,
So many things have come and gone, so many have passed through,
Well, change isn't always a good thing, it damages memories too,
So if it ain't broke, don't fix it, that's my advice to you.

Scott Rollo.

Magical High Row

Memories of magic

I remember waiting with my mam for the Corporation bus.
I was seven years old and bursting with excitement. We were in the bus shelter of which there was a long line along the bottom of High Row. I can remember it like yesterday, dangling my legs through the metal rail at the front, rain drumming on the roof. She'd told me the news on High Row. We were going to Thornleys to buy my tiny tears doll at last – magic!

I remember waiting on High Row while my dad disappeared down some steps to 'spend a penny' How I wished I could see below those steps, imagining a tunnel that led all the way along High Row to a secret door inside Joseph Pease. I reckoned there had to be a special place under there, why else would High Row stand so high and mighty over the facing streets and roads? It just had to contain - magic!

I remember as a teenager meeting my friend outside Dressers, wandering around Jean Jungle, ice cream floats at the Wimpy. We'd sit on High Row steps watching the meetings and greetings, listening to the town clock, eating apples from the covered market. It wasn't just a thorough fare it was a place where if anyone you knew was downtown then you'd find them sooner or later along High Row and stop for a chat.
It was - magic!

These are just a few quite unremarkable but very happy vivid memories of a place I thought would stay unchanged forever.
Will future generations have such recollections of time spent on High Row or will it lose it's magic?

Joanne Roys (nee Thomas).

The High Row legend

I smile when I see Joseph Pease back in his rightful place on the High Row, facing the town clock, I smile because it brings back happy wartime memories of my Victorian grandfather telling his grandchildren the story of Joseph Pease and the town clock.

Apparently when the clock strikes twelve on New Years Eve, Joseph takes out his pocket watch and checks that the clock is right. My grandfather would tell us this tale every year and when we scoffed that 'statues can't move' he would reply 'How do you know?' Have you ever been on the High Row at midnight?

Of course we hadn't and no matter how much we begged our parents to take us to the town centre, it was a definite NO.

A grandmother myself now, I recount the story to my grandsons, and they have examined the statue for evidence. Certainly Joseph has his hand in his waistcoat pocket ready to lift out the watch and check the timekeeping of Darlington Council.

Next New Year's Eve if you are on the High Row, just as the clock strikes twelve watch Joseph and see if my grandfather was right, and if he moves you'll know the legend is true, or it might be that you've had too much Newcastle Brown Ale.

Maureen Snowball.

A Fairy Tale of Two High Row's!

What follows was related to us by the sprite of that Darlington way.

Once upon a time, there was a pretty market town called Darlington in the North East of England, which evolved into a thriving place where people loved to go. I lived a happy innocent and undisturbed life there tucked away in a secret place on the old High Row for many magic years, spreading my fairy dust over all the humans who passed by. Then came the time of the big change, and from what I have heard via pigeon post it all came about on account of something called "growing potential". Anyway what happened next was a lot of men (some from far away lands), started to dig up my home so I had to temporarily move my fairy dwelling into one of the yards which was most inconvenient for me, and I expect it was inconvenient for the humans too, as they had to change their habits also. It was obvious that all this activity would disrupt the town for a long time, and in fact that things would never be quite the same again. I started to worry in case something quite precious was going to get lost, and hoped this would not cause too much dismay and shock amongst my hundreds of favourite human beings, who In my fairy wisdom I knew just like me had a real connection with the place they called High Row, and I called home. This special something that I feared may be slipping away was the thrilling 'feel' which only a very, very long established earthly place has, and it takes many human generations of people catching and holding dreams and memories to achieve this magical status. All such places have a resident sprite, and in this case that was me. My job was to watch over the folk who traversed along the levels of the row, and to bear witness to the part of their lives I shared with them there. It was a lovely task as High Row was a great attraction for many visitors, and because of this even though they were not aware of my presence, I was never lonely. So far as I know it was the only town around, to have a charming three tiered centrepiece, and I was ever so proud of it and used to boast about it to my fairy colleagues who were not so fortunate as I, and had to patrol less fascinating places. Oh yes I know it was getting a bit shabby, but it was still lovely and it worked really well and I had hoped when I first saw them, that these gangs of men were going to smarten it up for me. Instead to my horror as I helplessly looked on, they started to dig it up. The noise caused by the work and the digging disturbed the huge and rather unfriendly 'shopping mole', who until then because he was too fat to fit onto any of the levels of High Row had stayed deep down in his underground lair where he could do no harm and bother no-one. The men and machines toiled on, and as I watched them, much to my dismay I realised it would come as a shock to a lot of my dear humans when the builder's hoardings went back to reveal what had happened. They had slowly but surely turned the

The shopping mole
Created by Lee Hutchinson of Evolva

three levels into two, and the top one was wide enough for the dreadful 'shopping mole' to travel along. I felt very sad for myself as I knew I could not stay there now if I had to share it with the 'mole', and sad also for the future generations of townspeople and tourists who would not now get the chance to savour the former magic of the place, or have me to watch over them. Why would anyone even think of discarding such an attraction I wondered with fairy tears sparkling like stars on my cheeks?

On the last weekend of June 2007 there was a big party in the town to celebrate what had been done which I'm sure many townspeople and visitors (and even fairy folk like me) enjoyed, as everyone loves a good party. The party is over now however and daily life in Darlington goes on without one of its most charming assets, and therefore without little me the sprite of the High Row also. The 'shopping Mole' has moved onto my patch and he rumbles up and down for hours when no-one is looking…I don't think those camera thingies they put up can detect him anymore than they could ever detect me. Mind you I think some bloke caught him on a special new picture making machine a little while back so I'm keeping out of the way in case he comes back and snaps me… I've moved into Clarke's yard now and live in a nice little nook which I've managed to make quite comfy, near a shop which sells sweets so when I'm hungry I flit into there when they've gone home for the night. It's not the same now out on 'the row' 'though, as it seems at odds with the buildings and the other places around it, and there's always the chance of encountering the new resident Mr 'Shopping Mole' as he clumsily prowls around looking for things to consume, so I rarely venture there now preferring to work my magic in more familiar places. I hear they are developing a new oval heart at the other end of our town so that is nice, but I do wish my former home and my town's ancient heart, the old High Row could have still been here to witness it being finished, because then we would have had two very different hearts in one town which would have been wonderful. I would have encouraged Mr 'Mole' to move to the oval heart 'though, as I think it would have suited him better, and I could have been left in peace to weave my spells and take care of my humans here. Ah well that dream can never come true for me now, so I suppose there's nothing else for me to do except try to keep peoples feelings and memories alive for them, because they are what really matter. I do hope that 'Mole' will be very careful with my old home now that he's emerged onto the top of High Row however, because he is so heavy that if he falls off he could topple over the WHOLE of the town. I'll just have to try and conjure up a magical balancing trick to try to keep him steady, but I am such a little fairy and he is such a huge mole that it will take some doing. Well that is all the fantastical magical gossip I have for you for now, so as in all good fairy stories when they come to an end the question that must be asked about those who featured in them is "will they live happily ever after?" Well dear reader we will just have to wait and see…but I do hope so.

This comes with fairy blessings from the sprite of old High Row.

Both fairy pictures created by Lee Hutchinson of Evolva. Permision to use them is from Lee and from Carol of Fairielicious

The sprites new home in Clarkes Yard

High jinks on High Row

On the Town

All week long was work, work, work,
I've never been the type to shirk,
The weekend it was different 'though,
Because Darlington was where we'd go.

I used to look forward to a Saturday eve,
To hit town with me friends Nige, Julie and Steve,
Starting in the Imperial,
We knew the drinking would be serial,
Then we'd move round onto the High Row,
And head for the Wimpey for sausage rolls.

But then High Row changed in body and soul,
For a while it looked a bit like a hill for moles,
Hey now they are laying paving from China,
I guess I miss the Wimpey diner.

Now the railings have gone from High Row,
My spirits have just sunk so low,
What are we meant to stand on to sing Auld Lang Sine,
Is this just a sign of the time?
Yes I used to enjoy going to town to get plastered,
Now all I can think is what a ...shame!

Karl Harvey.

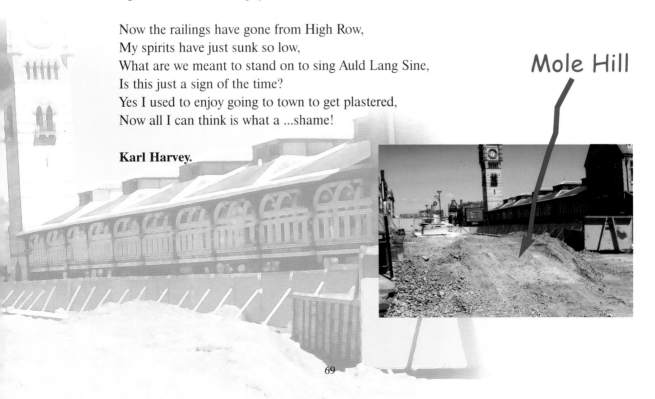

Mole Hill

Foolin' down on Old High Row

On the old High Row,
Many years ago,
There was Joseph Pease,
Looking tall and strong,
'Climb up you Fool,'
My best friend said,
I must have been out of my head,
As half way up I fell,
And hit the deck,
Years later at a party night out,
Loud music bright and gay,
We finished the night,
With a fish supper,
On the upper,
Steps of the old High Row,
It was always this way,
Back in those days..,

Goodbye to old High Row, we remember you fondly.

Pat and David Woodward.

The statue of Joseph Pease was and is impressive.
I see he still has his hand on his wallet, in his
inside pocket, safe from any pickpockets...

Emma Thomas.

High Row Occupants

This is an extract from Kelly's Directory of Darlington and Neighbourhood 1955. If the punctuation seems strange it's because it has been copied as accurately as possible to the way in which it appeared in the Kelly's directory for that year.

Blackwellgate to Bondgate.
Binns Ltd. Departmental store
Mechanics' Yard.
8 Home & Colonial (H. & C. (Retail) Ltd.), grocers
9 Swendon James & Co Ltd. Wine and spirit mers.
9 Smith James & Sons (Cleaner's) Ltd.
9 Thompson's, electrical engineers
9 Lee W. Chas. Lamp shade mkr.
10/11 Grisdale John Ltd. Costumiers.
12 Timothy Whites & Taylors, chemists
12 Hearn G L & Partners, surveyors
Clark's Yard.
14 Hodgson J. E. Ltd. dispensing chemists
15/16 Fox & Son. Hosiers
17 Gregg Bros. Tobacconists
Buckton's Yard.
18/19 Lipton Ltd. proven. mers
19 Peacock J. W. butcher
19a Cigars & Co. Ltd. tobacconists
20 Collinwood & Son Ltd. jewellers
Here is Post House wynd…
20 Hinde, Galt & Co. accntants
20 Darlington (The) Chamber of Trade

20 National Employers Mutual General
   Insurance Association Ltd
Martins Bank Chambrs.
Martins Bank Ltd
Darling, Heslop & Forster. Solctrs
23 Saxone Shoe Co. Ltd
24 Donald Anthony Ltd. outfitters
24 Fry B. C. & Co. stck. & share brkrs
24 Clayton Joshua & Deas. Archtcts
25 National Provincial Bank Ltd
25 Co-operative Insurance Society Ltd
   Darlington Burns Association
26 Luck & Sons, genl. Outfitters
26 Lea-Scott Ltd. dispensing opticians
Barclays Bank Ltd
Russell's Yard
32 London & Newcastle Tea Co, grocers
33 Philip (Drapers) Ltd. outfitters
   Yorkshire Penny Bank Ltd
39 Johnson Bros. (Dyers) Ltd
40a Pratt Jas & Sons F.V.I. auctnrs
40 Dunn's Footwear Ltd
41 Dressers (Stationers) Ltd
44 Bainbridge G Tarn & Son auctnrs
44 Provincial Insurance Co Ltd
44 Monument Insurance Co Ltd
44 Swaledale Cleaners Ltd
45 Pearl Assurance Co. Ltd

High Row in bloom

Darlington has always excelled in it's floral displays and done well in the 'Britain in Bloom' competition. We have always had a well respected, parks department which supplied flowers and plants for the Chelsea Flower Show over the years.

Colour

Gaze at those beautiful flowers
They look like a regal gown.
Run your hands along the railings
That embrace our Victorian town.

Marvel at the old buildings
The architecture a wondrous sight
Lift your eyes from the ground, up high
And enjoy this fantastic delight.

Something that never changes
Is the inner soul of the place,
Residents, shoppers and workers
Displaying magnificent grace.

Darlington has plenty to offer
Interesting shops to find
I will never forget the colour
Imprinted on my mind.

Ginny Harrison.

Picture of High Row, Darlington by Colin Bainbridge

High Row

Perhaps it was bare
But the bus stops were there
In places that seemed very rightful

And it wasn't all plain
As it had a cute train
With flowers that sprang quite delightful

I'd meet up with friends
And we'd buy odds and ends
And float from one end to the other

We'd no need to go
Down steep Tubwell Row
We just shopped on High Row with no bother

The old market hall
Had a certain rapport
And we'd climb down three steps for the getting

Then without any fuss
We could get on a bus
And haul our bags home without fretting

Grace Gant.

Picture of floral train sourced from the Centre for Local Studies in Darington Library

Haunted High Row

Ghostly goings on!

We all enjoy a scary ghost story or two on occasions like Halloween but do we have enough evidence to prove that ghosts and paranormal activity and the like exist? I would like to think so as it would prove there is a world beyond this one, but sadly apart from a possible encounter in my childhood with the hound of Throstle Nest (that could just have been a huge domestic real dog I suppose), which was supposed to be a harbinger of death (but we did have a family tragedy the following week), since then I have had no supernatural happenings at all in my life. Others have however, and two such stories are to follow this preamble and both took place in Mechanics yard just off High Row. There are quite a few ghosts rumoured to have connections with that area. A gentleman who used to work up that yard many years ago reckons that a few of his workmates had seen and heard inexplicable things and he describes one of those experiences in this chapter. Then prior to that just read the account of what happened to Bridie, my friend of over thirty five years whom I trust implicitly, who met a person who seemed real then suddenly vanished as she walked through Mechanics yard and you may start to question any scepticism you may hold. Other rumoured ghostly inhabitants of the High Row and its surrounds are (briefly) as follows. There are said to be about three ghosts in Mechanics Yard. One of them is that of a lady who was murdered in an upstairs room when people dwelt in the yards long ago… Another is said to inhabit the Quaker pub which is just off High Row.

Then there is supposed to be a ghost nicknamed 'Charlie' an ex landlord of the Bowes pub who sadly hanged himself in the cellar bar of that establishment in the 60's. In 1986 the then manager of that pub Andy Blair slept the night in that cellar bar and reported strange happenings such as items being moved about. There have also been

Post House Wynd
Drawing by Jean Kirkland

sightings of spectres in Clarke's Yard and in the building which is now Waterstones, but which Dressers occupied for so many years. The King's Head hotel has a resident ghost too from all accounts and in the past the hotel has hosted ghost hunting weekends. Legend has it that a tragic female ghost Lady Jarratt who met her demise by having her left arm hacked off by thieving soldiers when they couldn't get a valuable ring from her finger, used to emerge from an underground passage near St Cuthbert's Church every night and would wander the market place and Tubwell row in the form of a rabbit. She was said to be a benevolent ghost and had been known to help people, but when in 1938 Darlington Corporation removed the last remnants of her old home it seems she began to haunt the town hall where people reported hearing the swish of her silk dress as she passed along the passages. Other legends relating to Tubwell Row are that of the sound of a ghostly coffee grinder, the noise of which stopped as soon as the door it was traced to opened even a fraction, and the poor soldier who's ghost repeats his walk through Darlington in the dead of night to leap from the parapet of Stone Bridge into the river where he reportedly met his death.

One of the saddest but also the most fascinating Darlington ghost story dating back to 1745 is that of poor nineteen year old Cicely Kirby who met her long lost brother Barney Kirby (who because of his previous misadventures had run away to join the army and changed his name to William Trothie), in secret at The Talbot Inn which used to be on the corner of High Row and Post House Wynd. Their meeting was mistakenly thought to be that of two lovers rather than siblings and this mistake cost innocent Cicely her life. Another soldier named Sam Addy who had a grudge against Trothie saw them meet up, as also did Cicely's secret lover Jack Langstraffe. Cicely and Jack could not let their love for one another be known publicly as he was from an upper class family and she but a poor servant girl, so Jack tried to believe that Cicely was not being unfaithful to him and left, but Sam Addy did not. He stayed to watch his enemy William Trothie and could see this young girl meant a lot to him. Some days later Addy saw her in Blackwell Lane near the house where she was in service and he followed her and accosted her. In the struggle that ensued she fell and hit her head on a tree root. She was only unconscious but evil Sam Addy finished her off by strangling her with her own neckerchief, before burying her beside a hedge. Cicely was never seen again and no-one knew what her fate had been. Jack Langstraffe with heavy heart, not knowing why his Cicely had disappeared went off to fight at the Battle of Culloden, and by a twist of fate so did both William Trothie (Cicely's brother) and Sam Addy (her murderer). In conversation just prior to going into battle, Jack discovered that William and Cicely were brother and sister so at least he now knew part of the truth. On the battlefield he thought he witnessed Sam Addy who still bore a terrible grudge against William Trothie shoot poor Will in the back, but before he could do anything about it he himself was injured and fell to the ground. After the battle subsided he spied Addy lying injured too and crawled over to him and took him to task about what he had done to William Trothie and although they were both seriously injured the two started to wrestle right there where they lay on the battlefield. The pair of them were separated by stretcher bearers and taken to the field hospital and placed in the same dormitory, where at midnight a ghostly maiden bathed in a green glow appeared to them. Jack cried "oh Cicely" in welcome recognition but Addy screamed out in terror. Addy then related to Jack exactly what had taken place on the dreadful night that Ciciely had disappeared and confessed to his foul deed. As soon as he had uttered this confession he died. Jack lived long enough to write all he had been told down in a letter addressed to William Trothie who he had heard was recovering from the bullet wound Addy had inflicted on him. Once William was well enough to do so he went looking for Jack Langstraffe to see what had befallen his comrade in arms and although Jack had sadly died already he was handed the envelope he had left which told William all of what had happened between his beloved sister and the vile Sam Addy.

At least he now knew the truth and on his way through Darlington he called in at the house of Mrs Ewbank who had been Cicely's kind employer to acquaint her with the shocking facts so at least she could know the true fate of the young woman she had taken under her wing. Cicely's ghost was said to roam the lanes between Blackwell and the town centre until her makeshift grave was found and her remains given a proper burial.

So at least Cicely has lived on in legend and in a book writted by a Dr. Manson. I for one am very drawn to this story as others have been in the past which is why it has survived from the 18th century to the present day. Some say the ghost of the soldier who leaps from Stone Bridge may be linked to the sad tale of poor Cicely Kirby.

We will never personally believe that ghosts exist until we have had a supernatural experience ourselves, indeed some maintain that what we see when we are confronted with some apparitions are a sort of recording (something like a video) in the very fabric of buildings and such somehow captured in time at the point of some traumatic incident. I myself don't know about that, but I do feel that certain sites have a special atmosphere brought about by the fact that people who have gone before us have left their spiritual mark on them, and one such place for me was old High Row.

B.H.

The Memory Lives Again

Who can walk along High Row without memories? Sometimes these are other people's memories.

I need to make it clear before I start that I do not believe in ghosts … well, maybe I did not.

If I think too closely about an experience I had there just a couple of years ago, I'm reminded that High Row, and the Yards that lead from it, existed for many generations and bore witness to a multitude of incidents; some good, some bad.

How many people, over lots of years, have arranged to meet up on High Row? It's a popular spot. I hadn't arranged to meet anyone on the occasion I'm about to describe… but someone wanted to meet me.

One sunny summer's afternoon I was on Skinnergate and wanted to be on High Row, so I took one of the obvious shortcuts. I walked down Mechanics Yard. It was about 3pm and there were not many people about. As I approached the last leg of the walk down the Yard I saw a young man leaning against the wall, smoking a cigarette. We were the only people there and of course we looked at each other; being friendly Darlington folk we even smiled at each other. He tapped the side of his forehead in greeting and said 'Hello'. Of course I replied likewise (but without the manly tap). He then seemed to disappear. It had been a long, long time since I'd been down Mechanics Yard and I thought he'd backed around a small niche … after all the Yards are full of them. Imagine my surprise as I arrived at the place he'd been leaning against, only to discover there was in fact no niche, no corner to turn, no hiding place. It was just a plain, if a tad bumpy, wall. I couldn't understand where he'd gone. Oh well, I shook it off. But as I continued my walk he reappeared, leaning against the wall just a little further ahead. I registered surprise (just with a look, not with a double-take-hands-in-the-air backwards jump) and he smiled and nodded. As I was walking past him, he leaned towards me and spoke. His voice was inaudible so I moved towards him to hear him better. He repeated what he'd said but I still didn't catch it. As I apologised for still not hearing him – he disappeared! I was left leaning towards an empty wall. I looked for him, searching for where he could have gone, but there was nowhere. He really had just 'disappeared into thin air'.

One of the striking things about this man was his odd dress-sense. The best description I can give of him is that he resembled a sailor from a past time. I can still see him very clearly in my mind's eye.

In the weeks following that episode I tried to carry out research to find out who he could have been but I drew a blank. All I could discover was that two or three ghosts were thought to be resident in Mechanics Yard, but they were female. I will one day do a more comprehensive search to find out who he could have been and what he needed to say.

If this incident hadn't happened to me I would be too sceptical to believe it. But it was real and I now know that High Row has a lot more to offer than old buildings and quaint shops … it has a living, breathing history of it's own.

I since learned that at least one of the aforementioned ghosts of the Yard inhabited the Quaker Coffee House. This calls to mind another intriguing encounter. We were in the Quaker (now a music venue and pub), for a gig by Cathryn Craig and Brian Willoughby. They performed a song, a very beautiful song, called Alice's Song. The atmosphere was intensified when we discovered, just before they performed the song, that the place had its own resident ghosts, one of which the bar staff nicknamed … Alice!

Long may the memories remain…

Bridget Lowery, (nee Bridie Abraham).

The entrance to Mechanics Yard where Bridie saw her 'ghost'

Stories from the Yards!

The sighting of a ghostly jack-tar in Mechanics Yard reminded my father of Benny Bailey who lived in a house in the Yard. He was an ex-sailor who was employed as caretaker at Binns. Possibly if he was the spectre he was looking for his long demolished house or just patrolling the area.

My father was an apprentice joiner at Binns from 1934 and has memories of an ancient cabinetmaker there named 'Old Jim Patterson' who told stories about the town as it once was, He recalled as a young man that the police often collected drunken ladies of the night from around High Row's Yards on a handcart and pushed them up Northgate to the lock-up. He also told my father of a time when bulls were driven into Bondgate and tethered to rings in the cobbles awaiting sale.

While working at Binns the town rat-catcher made regular appearances. He used poison and a large metal spoon to despatch his quarry, and always retrieved the dead bodies from under the floorboards, as he was paid 3d per tail from the Council.

Wednesday afternoon was half-day closing in town and also saw football matches at Feethams. My dad and his mate Charlie Woods, an apprentice French polisher would climb to the top of Binns lift shaft and use a ladder to reach the flat roof. From here he tells me they had a grand view of the match for free!

Childhood memories he has of the area include throwing stones at the large hat perched above the drapers shop situated towards the north end of High Row, and the stink that came from the tunnel at the rear of the covered market where townspeople took their dogs and cats to be destroyed.

Mel Wallace.

P.S. It is common knowledge that some of the older workers in Mechanics Yard have told of some inexplicable happenings in that yard on many occasions in the past!

Pen & Ink drawing by Alan Watson of a view from Binns rooftop looking down into the yards

'Spirits in the stones'

A bow worn in steps
tells of millions of feet
going up high from low,
year on year the bustle repeats
up to and along High Row.

History embossed in every stone,
street, wall and roof,
a market town
of grand design,
look up and see the proof.

In quiet solitude
they look down to below,
through windows opaque with dust.
They call "we're still here,
we never left, can't you see us?"

Take time to stand and reflect
on the flow of spirit here,
present in all the yards.
Layer upon layer we add our lives,
walk through and feel the air.

Two ancient markets
with shoppers and stalls
are symbols of tales untold,
catch a glimpse from beyond your eye
of people from an old world.

An energy pulses from Northgate to south
of people, steam and coal,
catalyst of fortune,
renewer of faith,
adds life-blood to the soul.

The thread of our lives
entwined in our thoughts,
generations before and next,
add substance and colour
to present day,
vital heartbeat in context.

Be still at heart, eyes tight closed
wander your mind back and fore,
and remember
what comes this way in 'Darlo's' pose,
is flavoured by what was before.

David Thompson.

David says…
"I was trying to portray longevity and the fact that the town 'belongs' to no-one, as we are merely the guardians"

The spirit of Guru

The year, 1995. The girl, me. The shop, Guru Boutique. I had a good friend, with whom I'd just discovered Pulp, Oasis, and Ocean Colour Scene. The golden age of Britpop! It was 'Rock 90'in Clarke's Yard just off High Row for the posters, 'Soul Clothes 'n' Funky Stuff' for the retro chic, and Guru for everything else.

Upstairs was all about rock 'n' roll. There was even a hell's angel dog with a bandana (that was Lucky a wonderful and gentle Alsatian in those days, but now It's a cute little Schnauzer called Bandit) snoozing on the shop floor, below a collage of rock stars past and present that left not a patch of wall or ceiling uncovered. You could find some cool posters and t shirts as well. I remember when I first got interested in retro punk; this shop was my main supplier.

Over the years, we saved up for some really special Guru items, some of which we still have. For her it was mainly hand-dyed gypsy scarves and velvet handbags with mirrors. For me, it had to be (it could only be) my tartan bondage trousers that cost about two months pocket money and several 'Oh please, if you'll chip in I won't ask for a birthday present' pleas. Another great one was my purple silk Chinese style dress.

Downstairs was and still is the hen night bit, which we always had a bit of a giggle over then shyly ran out, and in the back room the Wicca/crystal section. The smell of incense and patchouli is a very heady one that I can call to mind even now at my computer screen. All the coolest greetings cards and ornaments were to be found there, along with Gothic dolls, delicate unicorn and troll figurines and more than a sprinkle of fairy dust.

At home I have a nature table, with a Guru-sourced block of howlite (anger management), goldstone (prosperity) and of course my hematite ring for courage and power.

If spells, runes and tarot are your thing, these can be found in the same section. When I saw the film 'The Craft' I immediately thought some Hollywood producer had been to this place.

The loveliest thing is that in ten years, and I'm sure many more before I discovered it, it's never lost that magical cavernous spirit. The heart of the shop is absolutely intact. It's never needed to adapt. Why should it? It does what it does well. Come, see and be enchanted!

Stephanie Rickaby.

Footnote from Beryl - When Stephanie sent this in with her piece about High Row I read it, enjoyed it and put it to one side thinking it wasn't relevant to this particular book even though it was a lovely bit of writing. Then all of a sudden I realised it was. The shop, its staff and its stock has kept abreast with the passing of time with only essential small adjustments being made and I think that is a good thing as evolving gently is the best way to go forward and retain and build on the past for the benefit of the future - so thanks Stephanie for both the advert and the wisdom. The building which Guru occupies is one of our oldest remaining shops in Darlington and is a real treasure. It has interesting little carved heads adorning the upper window surrounds and we love it dearly

On the buses

The town centre bus stops and shelters on High Row

Rickety and draughty they may have been, especially in the early days, and they really did need to go in the end, but for many years they served a useful purpose so the bus shelters all along High Row deserve a mention too! They have witnessed many scenes from courting couples sharing a first kiss to families alighting to explore the town, Saturday night scraps and so much more. They have seen changes such as being witness to different types of public transport and bus operators and saw the first Caribbean drivers and conductors at work in Darlington. They have also been a great help for the elderly or folk not good on their feet, who could find nearly all the places they needed to go to on High Row (such as a department store with cafes, plus chemists, banks, bakeries and optician etc.). Many used to pop off the bus there to do a few jobs, or shelter in them whilst they waited for the bus home.

My dad who worked on the buses for a while told me there was a particular conductor who was a devotee of some Eastern religion, who used to practice 'mind over matter' and would be seen on High Row in all weathers, even the most bitterly freezing day imaginable, with no jacket and his shirt sleeves rolled up, refusing even to use the shelters or his bus to get out of the cold for a while. His co-workers on the buses nicknamed him 'the last rose of summer'.

The smartest 'duck' on the job

Darlington's transport system has had a long history of running the population about. First there were the trams (both horse drawn and electric). Later along came the trolley buses and then the more modern single and double decker buses which I remember. "Clippies", drivers, trams, trolley buses and modern buses on High Row and the low flags, (where they all picked up and dropped off passengers on their routes), reflect another fascinating facet of our town. My mam Helen Irene Maughan or Renee as my dad liked to call her, was employed by Darlington Corporation Transport for many years (indeed when she first started the trolleybuses were still in use), and she often told me stories of what happened when the trolley's came off their lines, or she had to change her vehicle over to

The smartest 'duck' on the job.
Helen Irene Maughan

another route using a long pole to hook the vehicle back up to it's appropriate lines.

She was very good at her job and prided herself on her appearance and had the reputation of being 'the smartest 'duck' (conductress) on the job, as she kept her hair immaculate and always wore her hat at a jaunty angle and every morning put on a freshly laundered man's white shirt with a starched white collar and collar studs and black tie as part of her neatly pressed uniform. She used to work long hours and often did double shifts to earn some much needed money for her family as my dad didn't have proper work at the time and I have seen her come home totally exhausted late at night, only to be back up at 5am smartly dressed and ready to walk to Haughton Road where the buses were waiting to begin yet another long day as a 'duck'.

Irene in her summer uniform

When I was about fourteen years old we lived in Salters Lane South where my dad had got a job as caretaker at Springfield school. The caretaker got to live in the bungalow called 'Rockwell' which came with the job. At the top of Salters Lane was the terminus where the 2a or was it 2b bus would stop for fifteen minutes for the driver and conductress to have a break and when my mam was working on that route I would go there (as it was just up the road from our school bungalow) and sit in the bus in order to spend a little time with her. Sometimes as it was a circular trip she would let me stay on the bus and ride round the whole route with her which took us right through the town centre, past High Row and back to Haughton and then finally to the terminus near our house, where she would drop me off and tell me to run straight home. If the inspector ever got on the bus during one of these trips she would quickly issue me with a ticket. It seemed like a naughty and exciting adventure to me at that time and even better for the fact that it was shared with my mam. On one such occasion we were in the bus on High Row just about to set off on the second half of our journey when we noticed my grandad (Tom Fishburn), driving his horse and cart up Northgate towards us. He was contracted to take railway sleepers to somewhere in Whessoe road on his flat cart, which was pulled by a lovely big carthorse named Dick. On this occasion he was way off his usual run and we knew something must be wrong. As he got near we could see he was very agitated and we got off the bus to see what the matter was. "It's tha ma", he told my mam, "get theesen y'am, she's bad". That meant of course it's your mother, get yourself home as she's poorly, but grandad spoke in a broad and very old fashioned Yorkshire dialect which I loved. This was actually not an unusual thing to happen as my nana (Annie) was frequently 'bad' being a bit of a hypochondriac, nonetheless my poor kind hearted mam went white and popped me on grandad's flat cart telling me to hold on tight. "Go home with 'pop" she said "and stay with nana until I can get off duty". Off we went on the cart grandad and I, Dick's hooves clattering along past the King's Head and on towards the street off North Road where we lived, just like something out of a wild West movie. Years later I was reminded of that experience when our shop Guru organised a competition through the Northern Echo which involved people having to guess the time a pony (which was driven and belonged to a man named Sonny) and trap (which belonged to my husband Ray), would take to set off from High Row and complete a circuit of the town, arriving back on High Row where we were waiting with a stop watch and a big crowd of spectators to announce a winner. Apart from the driver the other occupant of the trap was a young lady named Margaret all dressed up in Victorian finery and holding a placard advertising Guru. I tried to locate the photo the Echo took to show here, but it was too long ago and I couldn't find it.

High Row when the Buses stopped There!

Photo sourced from the Centre for Local Studies in Darlington Public Library

The Caribbean connection

In the 1950's Darlington saw an influx of workers drafted in from the West Indies to do various jobs that needed doing including staffing our transport systems. There were now Caribbean people on High Row at the wheels of Darlington Corporation Transport buses with names like Sampson, Davies, Henry, Sandy, Joyeaux and Bacchus. These immigrant people brought a new spirit into the town and to me in particular. As an only child I had previously been a solitary bookish little girl and then I met the man known as Charlie Bacchus. I don't know if that was his real name as his wife was called Mrs Miller but that just added to the intrigue of this interesting person. He became the driver of the bus my mam worked on and that quarter of an hour stop at the terminus in Salters Lane took on a whole new meaning for me. Over a flask of tea and some food from his bait box, he would tell us tales of rum running and his other adventures in British Guiana (now Guyana) where he originated from, and show photo's of a magnificent waterfall which was in that country. How much of his storytelling was fact is debateable, but all I do know for certain is that he brightened up my grey world by relating these exotic exploits. Our families became firm friends and used to visit one another outside work hours and sometimes Charlie would throw a party in true West Indian style with ska music, dancing, joss sticks and lots of rum punch, and these fantastic 'do's' would sometimes go on for days. I met and became friends with his

Sydney's Wedding in1960
Malcolm Sandy was the best man and Charlie Bacchus stands next to the bride, (I believe he gave her away as her own father wasn't present) in front of him are his sons Charles and Philip. I'm the bridesmaid second from the left (aged fifteen)

relatives and his children. These sons and daughters were quite a bit younger than I was, so I would sometimes look after them if the adults wanted to go out. Charlie sadly passed away in 1963. My husband Ray and I were at the hospital when it happened. I am still close to this incredible family and Charlie's eldest son Charles organises his brothers Philip, Colin and Patrick Miller who are now all living in the South to make a trip to Darlington once a year on one of the Spring bank holidays, to catch up with old friends and take us for a night out. They often bring some of their sons or nieces and nephews too in order to show off the friendly town where they grew up to this younger generation. Sydney Sandy one of Charlie's relatives who worked here on the buses in the 1950's as well also returns to his "good old Darlington" once a year, usually in October, but he travels even further as he lives back in the West Indies on an

Island called St Vincent. He is over seventy now but still has great affection for this town, its football team and the people he knows here. These friends of both mine and of the town always say how fondly they recall the time they spent in Darlington and think of it as a second home. It will be interesting to discover what their comments will be when they return for their next visit!

Beryl.

The Miller lads and friends. In the dark glasses is Patrick Miller who is an actor and was our first Saturday boy at Guru - giving a hug to Kay our current Saturday girl. L to R are Philip, Patrick, Kay, Charles, Beryl, Oliver, Colin and Mark

We call this the 'Reservoir Dogs' shot - watch out for Mr. Orange.
Patrick, Charles, Colin, Mark, Philip and Oliver on their most recent visit - The High Row was still behind hoardings at the time!

Surreal High Row!

Some years ago I opened an envelope addressed to Guru which made me laugh out loud for its sheer madness. It was from a young gent from out of town who signed himself Steton Krawspracht. It was a request for us to send him by mail order a false moustache, as it seems he had purchased one from us earlier when he had been to Darlington and had grown very attached to it until he lost it, I think it was on the train to Leeds as far as I can remember. He began his letter by expaining how he and his friend Mr Truck Monday (who were both in a band, the name of which we won't go into here as it is similarly surreal), "two geeks from the Dales" as he himself described them, had a few months earlier made a trip to Darlington and discovered our "wondrous" shop full of all these young men's hearts could desire...this letter was a long one so I won't relate it all here...but it was so amusing and well written that I kept it for ages. Sir Steton told us of the things they enjoyed in Darlington such as watching people from the alley next to the Pizza Hut whilst stuffing their faces (with huge deep crusts I imagine). From this vantage point they had a good view of the High Row and all the activity that went on there. I sort of forgot about Stet until at Christmas we received from him a nice card with a picture of a Santa on which Steton had drawn a large black moustache and it all came back to me and we gave his card a place of honour as it was just so...well surreal. I started an msn group called Gurutribe and invited S K to join which after a long silence he did, and we never looked back on there after that as he and Truck who was also gifted with words used to keep us entertained. They eventually both went away. I think T M to a bird sanctuary (well that's what he said), and S K to New Zealand and then (having met a young German lady) to Germany where he still is to-day. Steton did once revisit our shop and that also was very surreal indeed and quite memorable if you appreciate 'intelligent' wackiness as I do. We didn't know what he looked like and weren't expecting him so when this auburn bearded young fellow with a floppy hat rammed on his head and a fake black moustache poked up his nose walked in I don't think Tony knew quite what to make of it as he had not been party to all the msn group goings on and Steton didn't say anything to re-assure him that he hadn't just escaped from somewhere except "is Bella Guru about?" So Tony just said I was out and wouldn't be in until later. Eventually I arrived back and realised who our moustachioed visitor had been and soon he returned and we met face to face. Colin made him a nice cuppa and I just cannot tell you all the madness that ensued after that, but I will say it involved the moustache, the seriously conducted business of him pulling a pair of large underpants out of his rucksack and popping them on over his trousers in order for me to take a commemorative photo of him in our changing rooms and a long conversation on 'spoon lore' (don't ask)! He was a lot younger than I imagined him to be, probably in his early twenties, but boy was he strange in the best possible way. We really enjoyed his visit and as long as he doesn't

The 'Pizza Hut Alley' - This really is Steton's and Truck's memory lane!

start taking it all too seriously I think he has a great future if only he could exploit that quirky brand of madness that he and Truck effortlessly project. I believe he may visit us again this Christmas, possibly Truck will come along too, and they will be very welcome.

This little prologue is by way of introduction to the email he sent us from Germany for the book…

My First Moustache

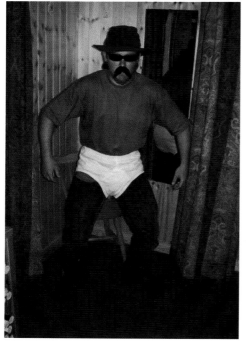

Steton in the Guru changing room showing off just one distinctive persona of his

Exactly ten years ago, I was sat on a bench on the middle tier of High Row staring hungrily at the then new 'Blood on the Dance Floor' album by Michael Jackson which lay upon my right hand. I was a young knave of fourteen, and therefore was not responsible for my choice of CD. As was always the case after buying music, I wasted the thirty mile journey home directing silent adolescent fury at my dad for only having a cassette player in his car.

I cannot say High Row was my only favourite area of Darlington, and despite my forementioned encounter with a bench, my posterium met but scarcely with the pavement furniture in that part of town. As a street, High Row certainly made the crossing from Blackwellgate to Bondgate possible, but this short fascinating journey was just one of many my friend and I used to take through Darlington. In later years, Leeds became the playground of choice for us, offering a greater range of unreasonable people with whom to jest, 'The Cockpit' and a far superior wall to sit upon for consuming fish and chips. It did however lack the character and breathing space provided by the town which is known as the Darlington.

On a recent trip to Leeds, Mr Truck Monday and myself were distraught to find that our fish and chip wall had grown to fifty times it's original height, and had exploded backwards from the cobbled street to form an entire modern office block. We sat on the hard pavement, our backs against the cold structure, 100 years of rain eroded comfort gone, the sun unable to penetrate the thick concrete and steel. It was upon this now extinct wall that the song 'Manshed Monkey' (a work in progress) was born, the chorus to this day remaining unpublishable here, but unchanged.

Can the changes to Darlington provide memories for the next generation? Who knows, possibly they can? For me, the bench that used to exist outside the Tubwell Row exit of the Cornmill Centre (a then relatively recent development) provided the perfect place for us to consume chips and fish. It had everything we needed, close proximity to the chip shop, seating for 3-4 people (or 2 people and two cans of Tizer), and a conveniently positioned refuse container (I presume from its absence that the bench also provided memories for vandals).

The most unlikely places can become legend. The underneath of motorway bridges, the space underneath a low balcony somewhere in Leeds that I haven't been able to relocate, the east arm of a dam in a remote valley and the alley next to Pizza Hut (full name: 'The-Alley-Where-We-Did-Watch-People-Eat-Pizza-Next-To-Pizza-Hut') are all etched in my mind. The old High Row is for many people legend. High Row as it now stands will maybe, given time become the background for that first bottle of Hobgoblin, that first game of Farkle and the place where countless youths will try on their first fake moustache.

Steton Krawspracht - Germany.

Footnote from Beryl: Well that was a bit of a surprise inclusion I think most of you will agree - nevertheless it is yet another real experience connected with that versatile place Darlington and it's old High Row.

This is identical to the said fake moustache which Mr. Krawspracht purchased from us on his first foray into Guru when he visited Darlington from his home in the Dales. I think he is onto his 4th version of it now as he keeps losing them...

A little bit 'off the wall' also is the fact that our very good friend Gary Dowson (Dowie), and some of his mates collect surreally odd sunglasses. The more strange the better and at present the Edna Everidge variety and Elvis specs are the ones most in favour.

Historic High Row

Copyright The Francis Frith Collection, SP35QP

Background photo sourced from the Darlington Centre for Local Studies in Darlington Public Library

High Row

High Row you have been here for a hundred years
So now that it's all changed we will shed some tears
No one could forget you and how you once were
Going through changes year after year
Yes there's been changes but much remains the same
The history of Darlington will depict High Row's fame
With Pease monument still standing tall
Still looking so proud, watching over us all
The Kings Head Hotel is also still around
Still serving Darlington, still rooms to be found
We've also the Market Place which hasn't changed much
Still bringing in punters never losing it's touch
Then there's the Town Clock still standing so high
Yes, the spirit of High Row for us will never die
You started out serving the old horse and cart
Then along came the tramway which was only the start
The start of our future which is now sadly your past
But our memories of you were built to last
Though you've officially changed, seen never again
In all of our hearts you'll always remain

Helen Sear.

In a Person's Footsteps

1875, Darlington was given it's milestone of history
Joseph Pease's statue was positioned with pride
At the northern end of High Row
There in history he remains our permanent guide
Described as keeping a protective eye
His achievements I hope will never die

He looks over the comings and goings along High Row
The life force of Darlington did once sow
Darlington's strength, our Victorian Railway Heritage
The Stockton and Darlington Railway Age
Surpassed against transport systems of the world
All proposals moved forward and successfully hurled

Generations come and go, but do they really know
Who was responsible for the making of High Row?
The inheritance we can find if we open our mind
Look on, it's not that hard to find

So mark your busy hour
As you look over towards the clock tower
Descending down the tier of steps leaving High Row
It's now time to leave your piece of history
My statue standing proud against all the crowd
'So off you go all friends and foe'

Sue Liddell.

What does the High Row mean to me?

In the past working on the land I have felt a particular affinity to my area – Darlington. However, it was only through doing my family tree that I understood how deep my roots were entrenched in Darlington and its area. I found that my family had probably originated in the Haughton area and had continued to live in that same area to the present day. No wonder then that I had felt torn from my roots when my husband and I had to leave Darlington to find work in Scotland. My own family progressed from being farmers to market gardeners in the 1840's and began to supply and sell vegetables to the burgeoning and booming town of Darlington. Indeed my family the Robinson's were among the first stall holders in the newly built covered market of 1864. Into the 20th century the family supplied fresh daily vegetables to not only the retail but wholesale trades, supplying the naffi's during the war and the schools during peace time. In turn I too started my working days attending the stalls in the Darlington covered market. The market then seemed like a happy family as everyone knew one another and I have happy memories but times change and the supermarkets having killed out trade in vegetables, I have now diversified into teaching local history at The Darlington W. E. A. and now do guided walks for Darlington Council. I am very proud of Darlington and its achievements in the past and I enjoy finding out more about the town and its inhabitants such as Samuel Tuke Richardson who worked and lived at Backhouses Bank on High Row. When not working as a bank clerk he filled in his time drawing horses, people and the coaches that he loved, also giving us insight into Quaker life in the late Victorian period. The High Row then and now is the heart and character of Darlington. If Tuke Richardson returned today he would recognise his High Row in outline but perhaps in lament the loss of its small market town appeal.

Jean Kirkland.

Pre 1901 High Row - A wide sloping featureless space when not being used for cattle and poultry markets.

High Row 1936 The Jarrow March

Were you on High Row on the morning of October 8th 1936. It was a Thursday and the interested shoppers were watching 200 disciplined marchers from Jarrow striding by with gusto.

Darlington had nowhere near the 75% unemployment being experienced in Jarrow but sympathy was felt and applause and shouts of encouragement were heard. Overnight stops at Chester le Street and Ferryhill as well as Darlington were now behind them and Northallerton the next. They sang, 'It's a long way to Tipperary' but they also knew it was a long way to their ultimate destination, The House of Commons, London.

They made it. Were well received in every town and presented their petition calling on the Government to do something.

They came home by train passing through Darlington faster than before. As usual the Government did nothing until Hitler became such a threat that Britain needed steel and ships and then the town of Jarrow was busy and there was hard earned money in pockets.

Allan Newman.

The Parade 1967

I had only been a Darlingtonian for a year but had been fortunate to become a friend of the Mayor Ald Alec Porter. His year of office was a splendid one and all the centenary events, including the visit of H.M. The Queen were excellent.

On the 2nd September 1967 together with many hundreds I stood on High Row to watch the carnival procession pass through and be judged. The road signs showed that this was the main road to the North. The crowd were neatly, almost formally dressed and good humoured with only an odd constable stationed to be of assistance. Innocent days.

The Market frontage looked smart and the town hall clock, as always, was a major focal point.

The ex-Major Alec Porter is still with us and can reflect on that magnificent year and look at the new High Row with possibly mixed feelings

Allan Newman.

High Row Remembered

The first visit to High Row that I remember was when just before Xmas in 1942, I was brought there from one of the Armoured Corps training regiments at Catterick to purchase from Dressers materials to make some posters of decorative (and highly improbable!), 'Coats of Arms' to adorn the Troopers' Mess.

My first thought was that someone had transplanted a sea-side promenade lock, stock and barrel! In later years I discovered that many of my HGV driving friends had gained the same impression the first time they drove through the town on the old A1 trunk road. They also remembered this town by "the lovely flowered roundabouts"!

There is a connection on High Row with another town I dearly love: one of the Banks has on its frontage some beautiful Cornish Red Granite pillars. I was in the Town Museum at Helston one time, and saw what on enquiry proved to be a photo of these pillars being loaded for shipment from the then port of Helston, prior to it becoming land-locked by the formation of the Looe Bar by a great storm!

E.A.J.B., (John) has many interests, just one being the appreciatioon of real ale and has a special corner at 'The Tap and Spile' pub

Another memory is of the Salvation Army Band forming up there in front of us, the Civil Defence Corps to play for our marching on Mayor's Sunday and other parades. These used to be quite impressive occasions, with other Services, both voluntary and otherwise, being represented.

I suppose I shall get used to the new situation, but will all the same remember with a touch of sadness the old High Row in all its Victorian splendour.

E.A.J.B.

The 'tribes' of High Row

By the 50's had got under way a phenomenon had occurred called the teenager and after that a fascinating variety of subcultures developed to shock and to change straight laced society. Some of these 'tribes' were so important to those who were drawn to them, that in a lot of cases, once people identified with these alternative cultures they stayed loyal to the lifestyles which went with them for many years, and in some cases for ever. First it was the ted's in their amazing drapes and thick crepe soled shoes, then came the time of the mod's (with their sharp looks and parkas and scooters) and the rocker's (some of the latter of which graduated into that indestructible brotherhood the biker's, 'cos usually once you are a biker you stay a biker for life). With immigration from the Caribbean came the rude boy culture and its British counterpart the shiny booted skinhead's. Ideas from America

Remember 'The Young Ones'?
Well the following are the real ones...

turned many young artistic people on to the hippy lifestyle. Sweet soul music, rockabilly, prog rock and heavy metal all had huge followings too, and of course in the 70's there sprang up the disco generation. Then along came the punks to upset the applecart yet again. All of these sub-divisions (which many regarded as dangerous and decadent), would have been unthinkable even in the relatively modern world back in the years just before and just after the second world war, as everyone then was simply concentrating on surviving the upheaval that event had caused. That was still a time when the young were expected to be carbon copies of their parents in waiting.

Apart from the iconic cultures just mentioned there are some other styles which emerged later, usually born out of musical tastes that people identified with; some of that music included heavy rock, northern soul, two tone, new romantic etc. Add to all the previously mentioned a fully fledged and enduring goth movement, more recently followed by skateboarders, and emo's. My own opinion is that if a person wants to identify with any chosen community that is fine as long as they are decent human beings too, as that is all that matters in the end. It's actually more worrying that there seem to be too many people who only aspire to consumerism but we won't get into that debate here. Hopefully all the main 'tribes' have been included up to the time of writing this, but there are always in addition to all the aforementioned, those who don't identify with any particular group and just do their own thing, or skirt the fringes of many subcultures as interested onlookers without actively becoming part of them. It's great to just be yourself an individual, just as it's great to be part of a tribe. Some manage to combine the two things very successfully for life, while others embrace a tribe simply as a passing phase and then put it behind them as easily as they had become part of it in the first place.

In some towns, often with a more sprawling urban looking environment or a problem inner city area (though not always Brighton beach being one example), there has been serious conflict between and damage done by some of these groups of people. Over the last few decades here in Darlington alternative lifestyles seem to have been more accepted than in a lot of other towns, and have managed to live quite happily alongside the more traditional elements of the town. I wonder how much that had a lot to do with the compactness and the 'look' and 'feel' of the place? To stride along the top level of High Row in years gone by with your mates, regardless of which group of those already mentioned you belonged to, must have felt indeed like you occupied (at least for those few minutes that it took to traverse it), a true tribal high ground and that you didn't need to prove a thing because most of the townspeople you encountered already knew who you were and what you were about.

Ellen. From the Guru Catalogue 1991

Perhaps that is why representatives from all these 'tribes' have at some point been seen on, or in the vicinity of, our High Row (remember how our local bikers used to occupy the steps of

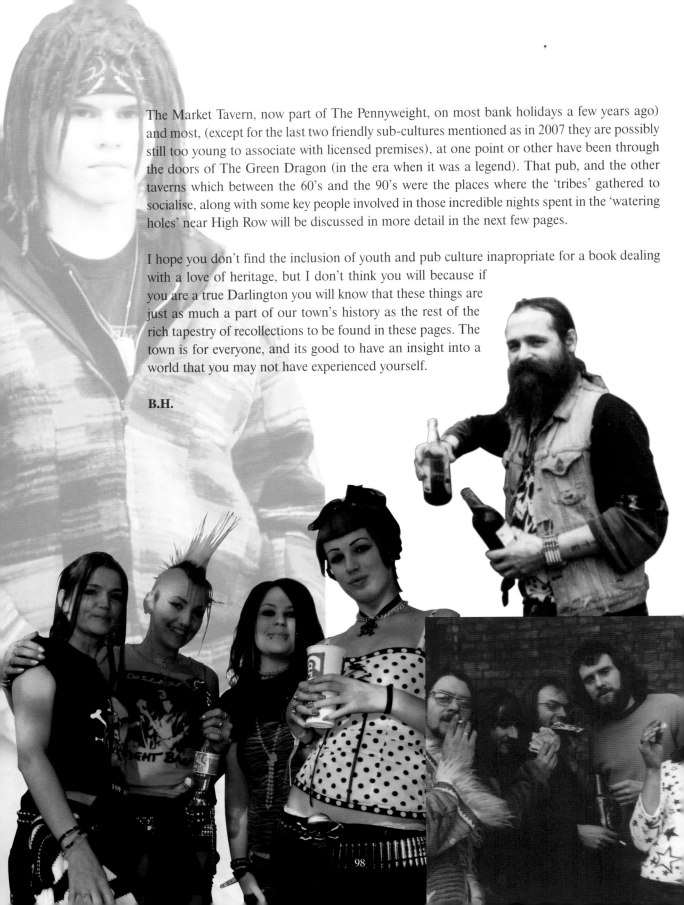

The Market Tavern, now part of The Pennyweight, on most bank holidays a few years ago) and most, (except for the last two friendly sub-cultures mentioned as in 2007 they are possibly still too young to associate with licensed premises), at one point or other have been through the doors of The Green Dragon (in the era when it was a legend). That pub, and the other taverns which between the 60's and the 90's were the places where the 'tribes' gathered to socialise, along with some key people involved in those incredible nights spent in the 'watering holes' near High Row will be discussed in more detail in the next few pages.

I hope you don't find the inclusion of youth and pub culture inappropriate for a book dealing with a love of heritage, but I don't think you will because if you are a true Darlington you will know that these things are just as much a part of our town's history as the rest of the rich tapestry of recollections to be found in these pages. The town is for everyone, and its good to have an insight into a world that you may not have experienced yourself.

B.H.

The Dragonites

Public houses have through the ages been very vital social centres such as coaching houses, town and village pubs and local hostelries where people meet up to relax and catch up on what's happening, as well as in some cases dens of iniquity. The Green Dragon in Post House Wynd, Darlington was for many years both social centre AND a bit of a 'den' to many varied people. The front windows of the pub were of frosted glass with a dragon etched into each of them and there was a large cut out dragon which was made of plywood and painted green on the very back wall of the lounge, which for many years watched over all sorts of going's on. It was a 'real' pub where

The outside of The Green Dragon 1991

old gents in flat caps would sit in the earlier part of the evenings with a pint of beer or two, reading the paper and chatting to their friends, and elderly ladies all done up in their lipstick and bits of jewellery did the same over a glass of port and lemon or a Guinness or something similar whilst a few serious drinkers would while away their days at the bar. Gradually as the evening drew on the clientele would change to include long haired rock fans clad in denim and patches, even longer haired hippies colourfully attired, bikers with leather bike jackets and waistcoats and tattoos, musicians, rugby lads (especially when the lovely Gail was behind the bar as her boyfriend was a rugby man), a few more hard drinkers and a band of tough looking men who everyone treated with respect known simply as 'the Scoops', plus girls and boys of all sorts out on the 'pull'. There were always a few of 'the lads' in on a regular basis and especially at weekends such as Stuart, Gary, Smarty, Billy, Pete, Nellie, Col and of course Gary Gilbert regaling all present with a run down of the latest sci-fi movie or his latest trip abroad. There were some rather more nefarious characters hanging around too, but that only served to make the place a bit more interesting and exciting. All in all if you were a regular it was a friendly place as everyone knew everyone. Even if you were a newcomer, so long as you were acceptable all you had to do was frequent it enough and soon you'd be one of the gang, and you soon learned to know who was ok and who it would be better to avoid. There was always great music on the jukebox and there were some great bar staff all the way through these years. There have been many in charge of that establishment who will be remembered; not least the landlord I recall the most, Alf Brydon. When Alf was on the door, especially in the 1980's when he started to have his two Rottweilers on the door with him, anyone

The Green Dragon football team (1969)

who he deemed might be a problem who he didn't know just did not get in. His motto was "when it comes to problems it's better to stick with the ones you know". What many regarded as the 'golden era' for the Dragon probably ended with the exit of Alf and Chris, and Jimmy and Pauline (the dream teams behind the bar). There was a final party in 1992 to commemorate the occasion, and everyone present got a flyer with a picture of a dragon and the words "THE END OF AN ERA AND I WAS THERE" to keep (well they weren't the only words but this is a book intended for family consumption, so I won't be too exact!). It's all changed now for the people who ran the pub, the patrons and the pub itself. Eventually the Dragon was refurbished and they knocked the interior about a bit to gain more space and made it bright and light. Oh yes the Dragon is still a pub, and probably a very good one. I don't know as I don't frequent it now as it isn't 'my' Dragon anymore. To me 'my' Dragon was the original article that only a real traditional unspoilt pub can be, complete with all the dark corners, the occasional edginess, the mixture of regulars with their tall stories, unique brand of humour, memories and experiences and all that went with that.

What follows gives accounts of the Dragon and a few of other notable 'pubs' such as The Old Dun Cow at the High Row end of Post House Wynd which had Jeff Addy as its landlord for many years and The Bowes which could be accessed via Mechanics Yard where lots of young people gathered and rock music in the cellar bar was the main attraction, and others which were in the vicinity of High Row, the place where after these establishments had closed people would congregate to see who was knocking about to either share a taxi or the walk home with.

Colin ordering two pints - I hope?

Jimmy Smith the excellent barman at The Green Dragon for many years. Jim was affectionately named "bacon neck" by Graham Nelson (Nellie) one of his regulars

Who do we know in this shot?
Harley Dave, Dave Smith,
Jacqui, Mark, Dawn, Bren,
George, Moira and Andy

Chewbacca used to bring his
Alsation in with him!
A lad called Simon once fell
through the door which led to
the landlords living quarters and
nearly had his head chewed off
by the Rottweiller that belonged
to Alf & Chris which was
waiting behind it

14th July 1992
LAST NIGHT
OF
THE DRAGON

THE END OF
A @!;?/@! ERA
AND I WAS
@!;?/@! THERE!

Spot or T.C. (we're not sure),
Nick and Spider (Jude)

Jacqui

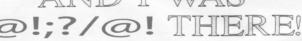

Girls just want to
have fun!

Interior of the Green Dragon one
Christmas in the late 70's. A very
convivial pub - the man with all
the beer is Peter Todd

Chris Brydon - Legendary landlady,
Karen Wigglesworth and some other
Dragonites!

Dragons and cows and other exotic females

I don't exactly remember how or where I was approached, (probably on a drunken night out in either The Green Dragon or The Dun Cow), but this stuttering skinny guitarist named Mick asked me if I wanted to have a go in his band, and being just made redundant from the KIX I said I'd give it a go. This turned out to be a three piece outfit, Mick playing guitar/vox, Keith on the bass and me on drums. We rehearsed in the back room of Mick's bed-sit, and this guy had a real P A. If I remember right it was made up of a couple of WEM speaker columns and a small but intricate looking mixing desk, all this equipment plus about ten miles of guitar and speaker cable lying all over the place was an accident waiting to happen. As Mick was particularly partial to the old falling down water it didn't come as a surprise when Keith and I walked in for our weekly bash-around to find the room in more of a state than normal. Story was, Mick had come in worse for wear one night and decided to have a twang on the old gitbox and duly tripped on one of the many 'snakes' on the floor, launching himself into and onto the equipment snapping most of the jack plugs in the mixing desk off, toppling the P A over, and demolishing the drums. The only real damage was to him and the jack plugs that were sheared of inside the sockets, oh joy!

We usually rehearsed on a Friday night or a Sunday afternoon. If it was Friday we'd do it as fast as possible then dive into Keith's converted Royal mail Morris 1000 van and get down to park on the High Row just in time to make last orders (which at that time was 10.30pm), at one of the pubs in the town centre. The hostelry of our choice was often The Dun Cow in Posthouse Wynd. The Cow was a lively pub to say the least. It was always packed out full of people you knew. There was hardly any trouble (there was no such thing as bouncers outside pubs in the 70's and early 80's). I was just a young lad and the things I vividly remember about the place are the antlers on the wall above the archway with the array of girl's knickers and bra's hanging off them, and the barman diddy Dave, what a character. The fastest barman in the North, running and sliding from one end of the bar to the other, hands full of drinks!

It was there we sat down in a corner to think of a name for the band. At the time we were all feeling a bit down. Mick, in his strange and infinite wisdom came up with 'THE DOWN TRODDEN CODGER AND THE HANGOVERS'. The name seemed to fit us perfectly, three young p***heads as we were, with no-where to go!

Another home away from home was The Green Dragon. If I wasn't in the Cow I was in The Dragon. To an outsider it was a den of iniquity; rumours of drugs, the occasional fights, bikers, punks and hippies all in one pub, but it had a great atmosphere. You could guarantee that if you walked into the place at any time of day or night there would be a familiar face or two. One colourful gentleman was Ted, who at the drop of a hat would start singing Irish folk songs at the top of his voice, a bit irritating at times but quite entertaining at others.

Some people would sit in the same seat night after night, Ted was one of them. I don't ever recall him sitting anywhere other than next to the jukebox opposite the bar. Another couple who were part of the fittings were Pam'n'Jim, always in the same seats and if by chance somebody was in their place, they would wait until they left and then claim their favourite place. It didn't matter that I was quite a bit younger than the rest of the crowd, or the band, I just seemed to fit in with everybody.
There was always something going on, from Irish singers to rugby team singsongs.

Along with its "reputation" of having bikers as locals came the interest of the local constabulary. There they would stand at the end of the bar sticking out like a sore thumb, with the new suit and a glass of orange juice. One time one of the bikers, Nick Lowther I think it was, decided to have a bit of fun with this one particular guy who was obviously suspicious of him. After being stared at for a while Nick stood up, picked up his jacket, made it known he was going and made his escape through to the other half of the pub. The copper thinking he'd gone gave chase and left by the main door to cut him off, only our Nick had only been waiting in the other room for him to leave and came back into the bar, finished his pint, and quietly left in his own good time.

A regular gigging haunt of ours was the Bowes wine cellar up Mechanics Yard. It was a tiny room with alcoves running off it and a bar to one side.

This was another one of my favourite places. Only open Thursday through to Sunday, it had a resident rock D J and on Sunday nights, local and sometimes not so local bands turned up. As usual with any venue some were good and some were not, and we had a bit of a reputation as being a hard crowd to please, probably because we all were into our music. The Groundhogs and Chris Rea's old band have played there but I didn't get to see the latter. Going back to the first gig we played there. I don't remember much about it apart from another band 'Jailbait' getting up to do a few numbers using our equipment in between our sets. Their drummer was a big guy called Mally Turner and he proceeded to batter my poor kit into submission. Every now and then one of my sticks would snap under the onslaught and I'd see the end of it ricochet off the wall or the low ceiling. All I kept thinking was 'my kit…another song and he's going to break my kit!!!'.

I couldn't believe how hard he was hitting my drums; anyway the assault lasted a few more songs and then subsided as they finished their set. As I went to inspect the damage Mally passed me on the way to the bar casually apologising for snapping my sticks. As I found out, that was the only casualty from Mally's pummelling. I think I only had one full drumstick left to finish off the gig with.

Dragons and cows and other exotic females

Andy Webb outside The Green Dragon in 1990. Andy's going to kill me for this as he ditched the long hair years ago... but this is back then!

Things started to go a bit awry with the band after a while. Mick got a bit despondent when we joined forces with another guitarist called Rod Young. I guess the idea of twin guitars was too much for him so he left. I was quite upset by this as he was my mentor in a strange kind of way, after all he'd got me into his band and I'd learned a lot of things from him, even if one of them was how to drink a lot in a very short space of time. To be honest he did look after me and we had some class times, but we didn't lose touch altogether as we frequented the same pubs and had the same friends. The last I heard he had a guest house in Scarborough, must look him up and scrounge a room off him for a couple of nights. After Mick left we did a handful of gigs, then even Keith felt he'd had enough and went his own way. Time to find a new bass player I suppose. Enter Carl Altdorfer, a rather large moustachioed chap who always wore a bright red leather bike jacket and never seemed to smile much. Never the less the band eventually gelled and we started to get a good following. We became the 'resident band' in the Bowes and would regularly pull in a crowd of over a hundred people, which wasn't bad considering the room (which was quite tiny), was only supposed to hold sixty. I'd try to make things more interesting by making small lighting rigs out of coloured bulbs and planks of wood.

We eventually got a friend to do the lights for us. His nickname was 'Fragile'. He was a quiet lad, always got jokes played on him, but he did the trick for us regarding the lights. The one thing I wanted to do was the smoke effect but as we hadn't got the necessary machine I decided one night I'd try and get the effect using talcum powder?? I sprinkled it onto my cymbals just before the first song which Rod intro'd and waited for my bit, then 1,2,3, bamm!! I hit the talc covered cymbals and 'WHITEOUT'. The whole place was engulfed in a fog of Old Spice talc. Everyone was coughing their guts up. Rod had difficulty singing 'cos his throat had dried up, and I couldn't see anybody. When the cloud had subsided the Bowes cellar looked like a Christmas card with zombies in it as everything was covered in a fine layer of talc. Bad move, I never tried that again, the stuff was coming out of my drum fittings for months after. Nightmare, but funny at the time – I wish someone had taken pictures.

Anyway that's just the tip of the iceberg, there was always something going on in 'The

Codgers' household. Oh by the way we'd shortened the name to just 'The Codgers' by now. I guess we weren't downtrodden anymore, we were just old f***s, well they were, I was still a young nipper at nineteen/twenty.

Andy Webb.

Footnote from Beryl: After this Andy was part of a successful band called 'Youngblood'. He was in the support band to an outfit fronted by Phil Lynott. I know for a fact he has many tales to tell of all the adventures he has experienced since those early days in Darlington but whether they are repeatable here is another matter. He has also featured in 'Moist', 'Barely Adequate' and several other Darlington bands with Stuart Goodchild, Trevor Gilligan and other notable local musicians.

A recent photo of 'The Old Dun Cow'. The exterior hasn't changed much since the days mentioned in this piece

Darlington in the dead of night!

Photograph taken from High Row by Marc Kay in the early hours - Christmas 2004

When nearly all have gone home to their beds, even the revellers from the pubs and clubs, there is something special and a bit eirie about being one of the very few souls out on the streets at that time. The whole atmosphere of a town is totally changed. It gives you a whole new perspective on your town and becomes a place where it seems like anything could happen...

High Row Christmas Eve 1972

Was it 1972? I'm not sure, so let's say, around then. I think we went to the Green Dragon, obviously. Then the Bolivar - old times sake. It was freezing. In winter Skinnergate is a tunnel for the north wind and we froze. We met up with Morts, Kenny, Phil, Stuart maybe, ran into Jim G along the way, lots of others too. The attraction of the Boli was that, well it was where we all grew up a little and it had a great jukebox. I remember the Edgar Broughton Brand and their engaging ballad, 'Death of an Electric Citizen' - Thought I heard a teardrop fall... me too Edgar. Steve and I then went to The Tavern in the Town, at one time a great pub (but like The Cleaver and The Fleece long gone). As we left the Boli Edgar and his band were deep into 'American Boy Soldier' - a suitably political number for the time but I did wonder whether there was much snow in Vietnam, as the song suggested. Who was Steve? A good guy as I remember, although I don't remember much more about him. We all had long hair then, very long hair, and I remember he was something of a Paul Rodgers look alike - needless to say I was impressed. In those days we all had these long trench coats, collars up, marching on. On the twenty yard walk to the Tavern we needed them, and then for reasons I have not the remotest memory of, we left. Heading somewhere else. The George maybe, looking for Mike, perhaps. Walked down past Binns and round the corner onto High Row. Just as we hit the corner the first few flakes of snow fell. Drifting down, big and fat. Harbingers of serious weather. As we got round onto High Row the sky streamed, the orange street lamps were just blurs. You could still see the town clock but at the far end, Peases's Statue was invisible, even more acceptable so was Woolworth's. A bus slipped by in slow mo, the light in the panel above the driver's window shining out like a torch on a helmet - 34 Hummersknot (no, not remembered, but it seems a good guess now). We were completely elated. Completely taken up in that high of the transformation of a sudden snowfall. Walking around in circles with our arms outstretched and faces raised, catching the cool flakes, singing 'American Soldier Boy', in a snowstorm on High Row, Christmas Eve 1972 - what could be finer?

Martin A. Conway.

Weekends, New Years (and the bunny run!)

The only memories that spring to mind about the Darlington High Row are New Year's Eve and the getting together of hundreds of people thronging the tiers, and leaning on the railings to welcome in the New Year. This can never be the same now.

Also there were the Sundays when my mates and I used to meet up in The George Pub, prior to going on a seemingly endless walk, up Bondgate, along Skinnergate, down Posthouse Wynd and finally onto High Row. This is what we called (sorry if nowadays this is non PC, but it is the truth) 'the bunny run' as we were looking for future partners. We would sometimes get lucky and pair off, either to Dipaloe's Coffee Bar or the Four Squares Cafe. In those days you were not allowed to stop in shop doorways, if you did you were soon moved on by the police, (who were more respected then). Sunday night was the highlight of the week for us lads, because friends met and had a good laugh together with very little trouble, and hopefully found a young lady. Maybe it is my age but nothing can last forever, more's the pity!

John Brass.

Nick Lowther on his Triumph Bonneville in Southend Avenue. Photo taken by Colin Harrison

The Darlington biker brethren

The bikers are included here not simply because they are one of the 'tribes' of High Row and can be remembered vividly from their presence there, but also because I like and respect them. This high regard doesn't apply to biker's en masse you understand as there's bad and good in any community, but it applies to most of our Darlington bikers. They had their HQ at one time in a street not far from the High Row and a lot of them used to frequent The Bowes pub which can be accessed from Mechanic's Yard and Skinnergate which runs parallel with High Row. I'm not really the best qualified person to discuss them as although I know quite a bit of what they are about, I realise that I don't really know the half…nonetheless I'll have a go. Our bikers are legendary and they have a sort of biker code which means they have all stuck together through thick and thin over decades and over that time they have certainly seen and done some things. They made the national papers many times in the 70's for various reasons and were referred to as outside of society. Perhaps they are but they have their own perfectly good society which works for them and the only reason for all this press attention as far as I can see was that they were (and are) outlaws in many people's eyes. They have occupied several doss's (communal dwelling places) in town including Winston Street, Stanhope Road and Larchfield Street. If you are known to them and accepted by our particular bikers then you are very privileged as wild impressive men of action though they are, many of them have hearts of gold (and they really know how to party too). If they don't like you however, then just keep away if you know what's

Haggis In the backstreet behind the doss in the mid 1970's

good for you. Fortunately they seem to usually accept you if you are a decent soul. An example of this was that when Dav would organise a trip to a music gig he would usually hire a coach and driver, and Frankie who was a coach driver (now retired) was usually that driver as he liked driving the lads and their lasses around and would always tell people that the bikers were amongst the best passengers he had ever driven, as someone amongst them would always take it upon themselves to clear away all the empty cans and stuff, of which there was usually a mountain, into a bin bag at the end of the trip, which meant that Frank didn't have to stay long at the depot cleaning the bus out in the early hours before he could go home. That doesn't make them saints of course and I'm sure they did all the down and dirty things that bikers do (and probably to excess), but it does make them decent people who know how to treat someone who's trying to do a service for them. I first got to know most of them from working in Guru because that was the time they had their doss in Larchfield Street just behind The Court Arcade where our shop used to be. Most of the bikers were regular visitors as we had things in Guru which they used such as joss sticks… My mam got on famously with some of 'the lads' mainly because she was one of those non judgmental people who took everyone on their own merits and they must have been able to see that. There were of course some total nutcases at that time and some of those were from out of town, but aren't there ever…on the whole however our Darlington lads in particular were very much ok with folks, if folks were ok with them. It was always heart warming to see my little mam chatting away happily to some big shaggy bearded, leather clad biker whom other ladies of her age would probably have run a mile from. These I must tell you were not your weekend bikers; these were the real deal and as wild as hawks and the leader of them was/is Jungle. One of the lads Nick Lowther was our friend already and had been for years and it was through him that we got lucky and started being included when there was a big biker party being held, often in a warehouse in Melville Street or more recently at Nestfield Club (my mam didn't go to these I may add as open minded as she was I think that would have been a tad too exciting for her).

Most of the Darlington bikers are big on music and so are we at Guru so it was just amazing to be present when the lad's decided to party to the likes of Le Rue, Steve Earle, George Thoroughgood or Lynyrd Skynyrd and the rest… Usually Haggis provided the disco or sometimes there would be live music like at Nick's 'thirty five and still alive' shindig when a band called Uncle Gilbert did the honours – I think? See that's how good their party's were as if you could remember them you just weren't doing it right. In later years like when Sue and Dav got wed, or when it was Tracey's 40th birthday Col Moss-Henry would either get George and a few of the others to

Haggis, Bopper and the unfortunate fish

form a band for the night and if he wasn't giving them the additional edge of his brilliant guitar playing he'd be doing the sound for them…

I think the lads are just great as they live it to the max and don't bother anyone unless they bother them. They live the dream of bikes and birds and booze and all the rest and they can rough it and adlib when they have to… Most of them have jobs and are willing to work as they need money to keep their bikes on the road as well as to pay for the necessities of life which in the biker world may vary from the things we think of as necessary. Life can be a bit tough sometimes as illustrated by this true story that our friend Haggis told to Colin and I. It was May 1976 and he and another bloke named Bopper were living rough and hadn't had a proper meal for days and were starving. They were up by the Tees this day and saw a guy fishing so they scrounged a fish he had caught from him and were so hungry that they lit a fire, gutted it and cooked and devoured it right there on the river bank. He also told me some of the reasons why in the 70's the real hardcore bikers and Angels had so many layers of raggy jeans on (sometimes as many as five or six pairs or more), but I won't go into that here even if it is very interesting, but I will pass on the info that you always wore your cleanest pair of jeans on the underneath layer nearest to your skin with the raggier muckier ones on top. Haggis (there's a clue in the name) comes from Scotland originally but he has been here for many years and is now very much a part of Darlington and he is one of the hardiest, brightest and most entertaining people I've ever met. All the Darlington bikers have very individual personalities and all in all I think many of them in their different ways are fascinating, formidable and great. Long live the raggedy road warriors!

B.H.

Some of the biker lads and lasses on a run and at a rally

Alternative Darlington

A little bit out of the ordinary.

It's not alternative in the 'trendy' sense I'm talking about here, it's the ability to be your true self whatever that may be and have your own special identity which you are comfortable with and that is what forms character. Every town has its characters. Some are locals and some are visitors, and I wouldn't mind betting that most if not all have been spotted on High Row over the years… so who springs to mind? Well a few decades back there was a shrewd little man with a lot of character called Georgie Forbett who led a very colourful lifestyle, and amongst other things combined being a coal merchant and fishmonger with great success, and started the first bus service from Darlington to Middleton One Row with a Model T Ford. Even 'though he was a wealthy entrepreneur he continued to live a strange but simple lifestyle in a tumbledown dwelling with his lady wife

Dav

Maude who from old photo's it seems was much larger than he was, and their child. The town has been rich with other ordinary and extra-ordinary people who were characters and if only I had time I could fill a book with them, but not this one I'm afraid as there is so much yet to be included.

Jungle. There is another mention of Jungle in Salvation Row earlier in the book on page 45

In the present day there is a man of legend amongst the biker fraternity named Jungle and almost everyone in town either knows him personally or knows of him, and most of them have their own particular story involving him which they will enjoy telling you if his name crops up. A few episodes which spring to mind are when he appeared in court wearing a red nose for charity, and the time he once let us use his fabulous Harley Davidson motor bike for a fashion shoot on High Row and all the motorists kept going round and round the block to get a better look at both the stunning bike and Paula the slinky model who was draped over it, or his flight on Concorde which he financed by selling his motor bike! If you dared you might ask him to tell you about the Christmas he spent plucking pine needles from his head…but I wouldn't recommend it…and so on! Quite frankly there is so much I could say about him that I wouldn't know where to start so I'll just leave it at that. There are so many other Darlington bikers worth mentioning too, and even if we can't name all of them here Scotty, Tramp, Dav (he of the plaited beard), Haggis (the man who's lost more brain cells than most of us ever had to start with and is still as sharp as a needle), Emilio (from Italy) and our mate Nick Lowther **have** to be included.

Vic Reeves even mentions Jungle in his auto-biography Me:Moir. That brings us to another local phenomenon the wacky genius Jim Moir (who grew up here and later came to be known as Vic Reeves). I can't help imagining that young Jim/Vic may have on occasion lead his friends 'the fashionable five' in a single file snaky line along the pavement of High Row, as they followed the Terry Scott look-alike with whom they were obsessed back then. I must ask Mark Tallentire who was part of that gang about this!

Even we three from Guru, Tony, Colin and I (about the time when we could be seen trudging home from work laden with bags and folders, and dragging Lucky my beloved Alsatian dog behind us) were once referred to as "local characters" by a businessman friend of ours, who upon realising his mistake blushed and apologised. He need not have bothered as we were quite flattered by his description of us, although privately we thought we looked more like a bunch of new age travellers.

That Darlo Vibe - the antidote to sameness!

This is Max, need I say more?

The sheer variety of human beings is a constant source of wonder and we in Darlington are not short of people who turn heads when they walk down High Row or anywhere else in the town centre for that matter, and why not? As so long as it's doing no harm being a bit out of the ordinary is a good and refreshing thing. People tend to be wary of people who don't conform to the norm and in some cases rightly so, but if there's one lesson to learn in life it's probably that whilst you should keep your wits about you it's good to keep an open mind, as it's sometimes the most unusual people that turn out to be amongst the most affable. Max for one as he scours the charity shops for interesting items of adornment and seems to have more weight of metal hoops and other objects hanging from the piercings in his ears and nostrils and goodness knows where else, than is physically feasible. I have mentioned just some of the alternative people in this town. There are also many others full of character that have emerged in Darlington and its surrounding areas from way back and right up to the present day. You probably know who they are better than

I do, but to write about them all would take too long. All I can say is that they all will either have, or be able to recognise and adopt that special Darlo vibe. I believe that interesting towns encourage interesting people and behaviour, and that predictable places tend not to. Although some can err on the side of being just too whacky or extreme to their cost I still think that's preferable to being boring.

B.H.

Some of the larger than life people of the town in recent years have, in several cases passed away far too soon. Here we take some time to remember them.

One character we will never forget is Graham Nelson (Nellie to his mates). He was, amongst many other things, an ex boxer, fundraiser for charities, singer in The Spiffs, Rod Stewart look-alike but you didn't tell him that to his face if you knew what was good for you, and the bouncer on the door of the Dun Cow and had an alter ego known as 'The Phant'. Everyone liked him and mourned when he passed away some years ago at far too young an age. He could often be seen at the High Row end of Post House Wynd doing the door steward job he did so well. Phil Ripley is another "one off", well known and much loved person who like Graham left us too soon. His widow Jane made sure Frank Zappa's music was played at his ceremony. Then there was Davey Graham…what can one say about him except that he loved life, loved music, and is greatly missed. We were fortunate enough to be in Hyde Park a couple of years ago with his sister Margaret to witness Roger Waters a particular favourite of his perform 'Dark Side of the Moon' which seemed like a fitting tribute to someone else who was taken from us too soon. Last but not least we should remember the gentle man named David Green who was a gifted artist, and spent most of his life conserving nature, had a special interest in frogs and newts and wouldn't harm a soul. David was sadly and for no good reason (as he would not have been carrying anything of value), shot by robbers whilst on a sketching expedition in India. He is lovingly remembered by all his close ones and his many friends. These people different from each other as they were, all had fantastic personalities and deserve to be mentioned as they are held in such great affection by so many. Sympathy goes to all the families and friends of the people mentioned in the section above and indeed to any who have had the misfortune of experiencing premature loss. There are others not mentioned here and many of you will know who they are.

The particular Darlington circles that all these people were known in would not have been the same without them.

Picture Perfect

This picture of High Row in 1991 was painted by Gordon A Hamilton ©

The painting above was taken from this photograph Anth Holdsworth ©

Punkin' it up in Darlington

The sight of punk rockers in the late 1970's on the classic traditional streets of Darlington served even more to highlight the message of the punk movement…the very contrast between the Quaker townscape and the brightly excessive youth style favoured by the punks screamed anti-establishment more effectively than any anti-establishment behaviour could and because of this in Darlington the phenomena that was punk was able to flourish and co-exist…

One of our first notables in the punk music genre was Mike Coles who inhabited Darlington until the mid 70's and then around 1979 went on to be part of (and design record sleeves for), the Malicious Damage label which gave us 'Killing Joke'.

A wide circle of Darlington's youth appreciated punk and so there would be representatives of rockabilly, heavy rock and just ordinary kids, who liked the fast, hard, pared down, rebellious nature of punk rock music, as well as the hard core punks with a political point to make.

1977 Britain was the time when the punk rock movement went nationwide. This was said to be year zero for music and culture. It seems that bands such as The Clash regarded both punk and reggae as examples of the true music of protest and this notion helped to bring people together through music in a way never dreamed of by the agencies attempting to solve our social and racial tensions. As part of this 'new start' bands like The Sex Pistols' advocated ditching nostalgia and adopting nihilism as they felt that the present system was failing its youth, and they had as their slogan "NO FUTURE". Although it was worrying to some people much that was good and refreshing came out of the punk movement, and in the opinion of many in spite of the upheaval it caused and its nihilistic warnings it has made its mark and actually changed the future for the better in several ways. Some even think that the punks with their relish for direct confrontation and the hippies who preferred peaceful protest, vastly different although they seemed to be, had the same goals in mind which were to be different, challenge authority, shake everything up, provide an alternative and try and change the world…it's just that they approached things from different angles and used different methods to arrive at the same ends.

What follows is a look at one particular Saturday morning in 1979 which allows us to see what it was like to hang out on High Row at that time with some of Darlington's punks, through the eyes of someone who was there…

Punks on High Row

Olly and Benk

Tetley and Bev

A Saturday morning in 1979 saw me aged fifteen and into heavy metal and rock music, up from my bed, out of the house and on the bus to town, to meet up with whichever of the people I hung about with back then were around so early in the day. I'd be wearing my normal weekend gear of Doc's, beat up denim jeans, probably a Motorhead t shirt and my well worn bike jacket. The bus would pull into the market place and round onto Tubwell Row. A short walk and I'd reach the metal railings. I'd go up the first three granite steps, cross the road, climb the remaining three steps and there I would be, on HIGH ROW. Constantly scanning the people I'm looking out for a glimpse of colour. Suddenly there it is. I see a splash of green and it's Dennis coming towards me clad in black crepe sole shoes, black bondage trousers, criss crossed studded belts, studded wristbands, an Undertones t shirt and his bike jacket with the Anarchy logo and the names of the bands Crass and Ramones painted on the back of it, all topped off with the green spiky hair I had glimpsed through the crowds a minute or two earlier. We exchanged our usual greetings "all right Dennis?", "all right Col?" and we're off to try and locate the rest of the Saturday morning gang. Our first likely port of call was Pease's monument, but there was no-one we knew there, then we turned up Bondgate and into the alley (Royal Oak Yard) where Robbo and Gaz Ivin were standing outside Target Records looking just as colourful and impressive as Dennis was. They were slightly older than I was, but there was no mystery involved in why I would link up with them instead of others of my own age who shared my heavy metal habit…it was because they were different. They dressed different, they thought different, they acted different, and people looked at them like they were some sort of alien beings. In addition to that they all agreed with me that 'the chief' (Lemmy) was great and that Motorhead were really an honorary punk band. So there we were Dennis as already described, Robbo in black and white skinny legged striped jeans, 'Never mind the b****cks' emblazoned on his t shirt,

117

Court Arcade in the late 70's.
One of the places frequented by all kinds of Darlingtonians or as
Irene (Mrs Guru) used to call them "all walks"!

black suit jacket, blue spiked hair and square shaped glasses with blue lenses. Gaz sporting black jeans, red bike jacket, baseball boots, a 999 t shirt and jet black hair, and me in my usual clobber. A few words of recognition were exchanged then into Target we trooped to be met by Ollie, and Dave Peacock. At that time Dave had a massive multicoloured Mohican haircut and Ollie had his hair twisted into long spikes, each one a different colour and both were just as outrageously dressed as each other in assorted chains and studded dog collars. Ollie was in a striped top (like the one Dennis the Menace wore in the Beano) and tartan pants complete with bondage straps and bum flap. Dave had on a top which resembled a string vest with massive holes and tears in it and bleached jeans with 'Stranglers' painted on them. These were the original punks and all their gear was of their own concoction, put to-gether from anything they could find in charity shops, rip holes in, scrounge off family or buy in street markets, and not in any way pseudo or self conscious. The way they went about things and the way they dressed wasn't mass produced or contrived, it all just happened and was their reaction to the smug, overblown, complacent times they lived in. I don't quite know how I fitted in with them, it was possibly because of the music, but I just did. Anyway we'd rifled through all the racks of vinyl records for the latest Clash, 999, U K Subs, SLF or any other interesting L P's, chosen and paid for our prizes and left, bumping into T C on his way into the record shop, wearing his trademark footwear of a Dr. Marten boot on one foot and a red trainer on the other. We muttered "all right?" as we passed him and he replied with the same pleasantry (we were men of few words). I could be wrong but I think T C was in Joe Lyonette's band The Bloodclots, and sometimes some of the lads would go and watch them practice noisily in an upstairs room up one of the yards off High Row. We six went down Bondgate and back onto High Row, checking the area around Joseph Pease's statue again just in case anyone we knew was hanging about there, and as there wasn't went along to sit on the steps just past Post House Wynd to watch life go by and see what or who turned up. We didn't have to wait long as soon we were joined by Dud the biggest Stranglers fan on the planet all dressed in black as a Stranglers devotee would be, which made a strange contrast to Benk who was with him and had on a bright orange fake fur coat which looked like it was made out of the stuff they cover cuddly toys with. It was decided that the next port of call should be the record part in Guru in the Court Arcade to see what they had to offer in the way of indie music and to pass some time with Stuie who worked there. We were just about to set off for that destination when we heard some snarley, snotty music. It was Twed with a ghetto blaster blaring out who joined us, so we decided to sit there on the High Row steps in

Kim and Manda in the Green Dragon back in the day....

the sun for a bit longer in order to savour all the pointing and mumbling and looks of disapproval and disbelief we were getting from the passers by. After all wasn't that what it was all about? The lads had to be seen by 'joe public' in order to make their statement…

The town clock struck 12.30 about the time we were getting hungry, so buying sustenance on the way (in my case a large stottie which the lady in the fish and chip shop in Post House Wynd filled with chips for me) and gulping our food down as we went, we did the trip to Guru (which was then in Court Arcade). We spent some more of our limited funds there on badges and punk singles, after that we moved on to Mr Angry's record shop in Larchfield Street which was run by Owen (who later had a record stall on the market), then finally ended up in 'Space City' a games arcade in Northumberland Street to meet a few more people who were in there already playing space invaders and the like on the machines in that excellent dive with it's walls covered in glittering paint. People started drifting off home to stash away the precious vinyl they had acquired to-day to be played later…

To-night we'd all probably meet up again in Stanhope park to do the things we did in those days, one of which was downing evil homebrew (sediment and all), and hoping we'd all be over the bad belly aches we'd probably have to-morrow, in time for the next Bloodclots gig at the Turks Head. During the week some of us would no doubt be seen back on High Row late at night preparing to walk home from either the Bowes cellar bar or The Green Dragon…

By some quirk of fate, after leaving school at fifteen seemingly destined for a life of working on building sites, I work in Guru now. I remember they took a bit of persuading to employ me as when I first asked for a job there aged about seventeen they gently but firmly told me there was no vacancy in the rock music section as Stuart had that job, and they didn't think I was suitably qualified to handle working in the clothing department…but I persevered and finally in 1990 got there in the end.

A lot of the people from way back in the late 70's and early 80's have left Darlington, but always seem to gravitate back to their hometown now and then…usually on bank holidays when some of them are back for various reasons and they often drop into the shop to catch up.

If anyone's interested this is a list of those I remember from Darlington's punk heyday, and if I've left anyone out or got anything wrong I apologise but it WAS over twenty years ago…not all of the people mentioned here were actually punks but they did hang out to-gether and dug the music. In fact if I had to give them any label it would be Dragonites!

Some of the punks and Dragonites

As far as I know here's what happened to them…

Jacqui and Dawn in the early 1990's. The girls look very different now but are still rebels just as they were back then!

Dennis (went to London and is still being Dennis - rumour has it that at one time he was employed by an agency to look after Lemmy's apartment).
Kath (think I saw her on the High Row recently).
Ollie (we see him off and on when he pops into Guru).
Tetley (she's around somewhere I'm sure).
Robbo (still into music).
Bren and Jacqui (happily married with a family).
Dawn (married with a family).
Rebecca (we see her quite often I'm glad to say).
Lisa (pops into our shop now and then).
Jackie (also married and has children).
Dud (?).
Benk (haven't seen him for years).
T C (haven't bumped into him lately but think he's in Darlo somewhere).
Bev Bowes (still got that great personality and works for Royal Mail).
Dave Peacock (married and has a family).
Dins (not sure where he is now but always wore a yellow bike jacket with Siouxsie Sioux painted on it).
Twed (doing very well I hear with many creative projects).
Paddy (?).
Mandy (alive and well, went to Leeds and is now living in the South I think).
Gaz Ivin (went on to join The Fits and moved to California where he's in a successful rock band).
Jayne Buckton (talented thespian married and went to London).
F-stroke (?).
Les (?).
Wilk (?).
Joseph (the hippy of the bunch).
Ben and Sharon (now have a daughter Mary Joanna)
Wally (now more usually know under his real name of Andrew does a great job as a youth worker and will always be remembered from the days when he knocked about with us for wearing a black second hand tail coat with a spray of dead flowers in the buttonhole).
Carol (I believe she's doing ok in the beauty business).
Joe Lyonette (now a local labour councillor and still one of the lads).
Vanessa (got married, worked in the tax office in Shrewsbury for a good while and is now doing a degree in Durham).
Sandra (lives in Darlo).
Helen (went to live in London, but after many years there may be coming back here soon).
Stuart (left Guru to seek wider horizons – married with family and is doing well – thanks for your job mate).
Gary (good to see he's still into music – married to Tracy and has a family).
Anth and Alice (not only a couple but used to look like clones of one-another when they lived here. They had a comic shop in Clarkes Yard and a band called The Magic B'stards, they later moved to London to-gether where Anth is now known as Charli and is in a band called TV Babies, and the stylish Alice has just given birth to baby Rosa Lux.
There were many, many, other people too but if I don't want to fill the whole book I'll have to leave it there.

Col.

'Punks not dead'
David Brunton heads for High Row in the early 2000's
Photo by Zara

High style on High Row

Sunday best on Saturdays

High Row on a Saturday was the place to meet
Then off to Binns for coffee – if you could get a seat!
We had a regular table on which it said 'Reserved'
Our waitress served us special cakes – with scones and jam preserves

The highlight was the fashion show, with models dressed to sell
The stores 'top numbers' to the crowd, who applauded each one well
All around the tables the models walked with glitz
And talked about the clothes they wore, the colour, price and fit

Then the fashion show continued with a walk on the High Row
Every lady wore a hat, with shoes and bag to go!
My grandma's hat was navy/white, red roses round the brim
My mother dressed in palest blue with petal hat so trim

I recall it all with fondness, though time may pass me by
A vivid picture in the mind that doesn't want to die
So ever I remember those days of long ago
When Saturday's meant 'Sunday Best' on Darlington's High Row

Ann Blyth.

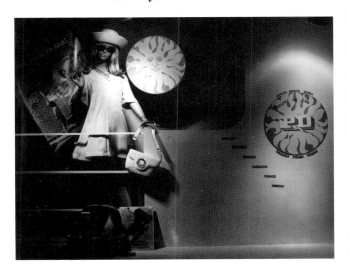

This was a fashion based promotion window for Eden Vale Travel which had a department situated on the ground floor of Binns and was created by the prizewinning Binns design team led by Alan Watson.

Text and photographs supplied by Alan Watson
©Alan Watson

Darlington - High Row

It was so pleasant some years ago
To walk along the old High Row
Good shops were selling this and that
One had a trade sign of a large top hat

The steps were easy to walk up and down
The Balustrades gave character to the old market town
Saturday morning was a fashion parade
With everyone in their best clothes arrayed

Then in the evening of the following day
The band of the Salvation Army would play
Joseph Pease overlooked a well ordered town
Today I think he'll be wearing a frown

Mrs E.W. Town.

Mrs Town's father and a friend striding down High Row dressed in the fashion of the time. 'Bogart Macs' and Crombie 'King Coats' were the ultimate in style for the well dressed man

Nostalgia

The High Row of the fifties when I was in my teens
Buzzed with elegant people, no such thing as stoned washed jeans

Joseph Pease stood watching as folks passed along the Row
Saturday was always the peoples fashion show

Ladies dressed in Sunday best stopping for a chat
Gentlemen in blazers politely raised their hat

Boy's home from Uni knew exactly where to go
Best place to meet friends, of course 'High Row'

Following latest fashion, girl's dresses stuck out miles
With yards of net underskirts attracting the boy's smiles

Time for coffee, chat about last night
Did you see those Teddy Boys, my what a sight!

Binns for coffee Saturday, Green Tree after School
Sounds tame and old fashioned, we thought ….pretty cool!

Rushing home at tea time, buses all in line
Running along the High Row to join the queue for mine

Market day was hectic, folks flocked into town
It was a regular social event, everyone came down

There were no designer outlets or fancy shopping malls
Farmers came to the cattle mart and met up with their pals

Their wives had a hair do came out with lots of curls
Collected their groceries, then lunched with all the 'Girls'

From Northgate through to Blackwellgate the traffic crawled along
How many can remember the route of the old A1

Joseph Pease has pride of place but is looking full of woe
Sharing my nostalgia for the Old High Row

Dorothy Wilson.

Luck and Sons. Photo sourced from the Centre for Local Studies in Darlington Public Library

Luck's drapery store - High Row, Darlington

The gorgeous red leather gloves

My great-grandmother (then Mary Elizabeth Rex) was apprenticed to Luck's dressmaking department in the 1880's as a young woman. When she was about to marry, aged 21 years in December 1892, she was invited by the owners of this business to choose fabric, and to make her own wedding dress. Her training gave her the skills to design, cut and make a wide range of clothing and to later dress her own family and furnish her home. She was able to pass on her love of good quality fabrics and sewing skills through her children, grandchildren and great-grandchilden.

My own early memories of the store were as a child (aged about seven) visiting with my mother and younger sister to choose fabrics for nightdresses, frocks and coats during the 1950's Mum would select a small range of suitable fabrics for the item in mind, then my sister and I would make our choices. I loved seeing the fabrics rolled round boards neatly stacked on the polished dark wooden shelves. There was an upper ledge to display dress styles alongside fabric lengths. All the shelving ran the length of the walls from front to back of the shop, and parallel to the long polished and hinged measuring counters inlaid with brass rules along one edge.

In the centre of the shop was an island counter inside which were tall units of glazed compartments and pullout wooden drawers for gloves, stockings, handkerchiefs etc. I still have a pair of bright red fine leather gloves purchased from pocket money during the early 1960's to accessorise a grey coat and dress (when I was sixteen or seventeen).

I moved away from Darlington – first to colleges, university and then to work in Cumbria and London as a teacher of art and design, specializing in textiles and embroidery, but returned frequently to visit my family.

Sadly the shop closed in the 1960's, It was taken over by Dresser's stationers until they too closed down in the late 1990's. After a long period of abandonment it has been rebuilt as Waterstone's Bookstore.

Irene Ord (Lecturer in Art and Design – retired).

The Lucinlux

I'm going for a Lucinlux
I'll be back at half past two
Don't worry about your dinners
You can finish up Fridays stew.

The following week on Saturday
The same thing happened again
I'm going for a Lucinlux
On the bus at quarter past ten

Each month as I got older
I realised what was going on
My mother was buying Lucinlux
There was something seriously wrong

It was a whole year later
When I asked my brother Pete
Do you know what a Lucinlux is
I think it's for your feet

No, I think its perfume
To keep you smelling nice
Unless it's a brand new type
Of American pudding rice

Even though I was still young
The strain was driving me wild
Trying to find a Lucinlux
Is difficult for a child

The next Saturday very early
After mother had gone to town
I searched through all the pantry
From every top shelf down

Will you ask our mother Pete
About the Lucinlux
I daren't go in their bedroom
Or she'll box me bloomin' lugs
I know they're all in there
Piled up on the wardrobe top
I'm sure the noise last night
Was them beginning to drop

Mother suddenly burst in
So quickly, it was said
Did you get another Lucinlux
When you went out for the bread

Well, yes I did thank you
It's a lovely shop to see
On Darlington's High Row
Further along from Lipton's Tea

One day when we've all got time
I'll take you through into town
For a little look in Luck's
To spend that half a crown

T Hughes.

126

Classic High Row

High Row and West Row c1965 - Copyright The Francis Frith Collection, SP35QP

Whether you are a fan of the Victorians or not they did know about construction, and how to make things look good and work well. This street arrangement deals perfectly with the slope it is situated on and allows for good people flow, easy access and solves drainage and other problems in an attractive but common sense way.

Usually it is we who traverse the pavements who look into the shop windows we pass... unusually Marion Watson lets us know just what it's like to reverse the normality and look out upon life beyond the glass window panes of a High Row shop!

The other side of the Window

Spirit of High Row. Is there any spirit left now or is it simply a space which people dash along to get from one end of the town to the other ?

Do people ever stand and look in shop windows or are they in too much of a hurry? When I started working for Binns in 1950 their windows were the by-word for good display. I was lucky to work there for I recieved an excellent display training and also had a grandstand view of the High Row. Not only a characterful place, but a place full of characters.

Top of this list was Mr Bryant, yes we addressed each other formally in those days, no bandying about with first names. Binns commissionaire set the tone. Tall, imposing, dignified in his dark uniform with the gold embroidered "Binns Ltd" logo on his peaked cap, this Boer War veteran kept order with a look, a tilt of the head and in extreme cases, a gently admonishing crooked finger.

Then there was the lady who regularly scoured the windows and if a customer took some time in deciding whether she wished to purchase a garment taken from a display model or if the sales woman couldn't find a junior to take down a replacement, this self appointed guardian of decency would come in to harangue the display manager, Mr James. Finally tiring of this, he referred her to fashion buyer Miss Steel, a daunting Scottish lady who quelled any further argument in her best "Prime of Miss Jean Brodie" voice "You maind your business and a'll maind maine"

After this, drawstring covers were made for the nude headless, armless dummies to guard passing innocents against possible attacks of the vapours.

Oily Olly, aptly nicknamed by the display staff spent his dinner time lurking outside The Fleece Hotel diagonally opposite, shiftily eying the heavily net curtained windows of Binns first floor fitting rooms. It was time wasted, for only after the velvet curtains had been closed was the light switched on by the sales assistant. No oily overalled workman was going to be allowed even a glimpse of her customer clad in her industrial strength Spirella corsets.

Every Thursday the Walker Sisters hit town. Five girls, not one any less glamorous than her siblings. Figures like Jane in the "News of the World" comic strip, hair either piled high or in a swinging page boy roll, they strode along in their high heels, seemingly un-aware of the stir that

The other side of the Window

they caused - and their dresses! made by their mother fitted perfectly.

They bought their material in Binns. Even fabric saleswoman Miss Hubter, no mean seamstress herself, marvelled that so much effect could be achieved by so little yardage. They were fifty years ahead of their time.

Two or three times a week the coffee laidies met. In their Van - Dal shoes, servicable stockings, Hebe or Windsmoor suits, hats by Mitzi Lorenz, carrying frame handbags by Holmes of Norwich in their kid gloved hands, they alighted from trolleys and buses to gather in their favourite haunts to discuss who knows what. Where are the likes of them to be found now, those souls of respectability who dressed so decently and oh, so dully.

What would they make of the bulging bare midriffs, tracksuits and trainers of today's High Row? Brought up to believe that only "common" people ate in the street, what would they think of the greasy food wrappings so carelessly dropped on the multi million pound replacement of the pavement they had trod with such decorum.

From our grandstand, the display team watched the world go by, for in those days

Beautiful People! Alan & Marion Watson and Maurice James (the display staff at Binns Darlington at a staff 'do' in the 60's). Alan is the young upstart Marion just had to marry when he was promoted instead of her. They make a lovely couple so it was just as well she did. Photo by A. Watson

the A1 went through the heart of the town. We saw impressive military parades, someone told us that the D.L.I. were the fastest marching regiment and I've never doubted it.

We saw the Royal Marines Band immaculately turned out in colourful uniforms. We watched the newly sand coloured camouflaged tanks and lorries rolling past en-route to solve the Suez Crisis. We saw royalty enter The old Town Hall opposite and wondered if they understood the builder/town councillor when he talked about "chimblies". There was indeed an impressive variety of chimneys above the yards off High Row. My husband did a drawing of them.

The other side of the Window	Oh yes, I even got my husband from Binns windows. He came from Art College as an apprentice and I trained him. When Mr James left, this upstart was promoted over my head and I wasn't having that, so I married him out of pique.

Fifty one years later we try to remember what was where - the Home and Colonial Grocery. The butchers where I went to collect Mr James' two lamb cutlets for his batchelor Sunday lunch, Luck's Drapery Store where cashiers sat in a high pulpit like structure receiving payment and sending change whizzing back along wires in little cylinders.

Were these really the good old days? Well yes and no. We miss the standards but not the stuffiness. Now, as then, it is people not surroundings that create the spirit - that companiable atmosphere composed of good manners, cheeriness, kindness, courtesy and tidyness.

Let's work on it.

Marion Watson.

Staring through a Darlington window!

Sometimes I look out but there's nothing there,
My thoughts use my eyes and I appear to stare.
The vision before me is no more,
Dreams cloud the scene of what's in the fore.
In view I see my person, the feeling is quite strange,
A plan of action revealed, my life it is to change.
I'm listening don't worry,
I'll answer as well,
But reality is masked by a more interesting tale.
A tale of success, achievement and wealth,
I take care in that dream,
Approaching with stealth.
But, back to reality, the present, real time,
The pressure of work tires me out, but I'm fine.
I'm happy don't worry, no longer stressed,
All my family are healthy
All concerns are addressed,
We all have dreams
Sometimes good, sometimes bad,
But the best dream of all
Is the life that I've had.

Graeme Halloway.

More memories...

Happiness & heartache - Elaine's memories...

Just like any other Darlingtonian, the High Row has been a background in my life for as long as I can remember, had I known that it was only to be part of my life for thirty seven years, I would have tried to savour many more memories than I hold and regret with hindsight that from the day I was born in this town, to the final moments of it's existence I never had my photograph taken on the beautiful steps against the black railings. Now sadly I have missed my chance and the only photograph I hold is in my head, with my memories.

My childhood memories are a jumble of Saturday mornings holding mam's hand, whilst winding through the endless stream of shoppers on the top tier of the High Row. We would walk from Blackwellgate around the corner of Binns department store where I would embark on a journey of pure enjoyment only a child would understand on a boring shopping day, adults of course being too busy with the task in hand to notice. It began with the smell of freshly ground coffee wafting through the door of the food hall in Binns, I would the gaze at the displays in the windows as we rounded the corner to the High Row. As we turned, I would then be hit with another smell wafting from the front doors, a mixture of the expensive perfumes which were sold at the front of the store, on various counters by perfectly made up, immaculate ladies.

From this point I remember various buildings and shops which were important to me in some way. There was the wonder of Dressers, my pace would quicken as we came closer to that shop wondering if there was another huge 'Lego' display in the front window to guess the number of bricks on. Barclays Bank seemed a large imposing building, to a small child almost on a cathedral scale, in fact looking at it as an adult it is still a grand affair. There was the Ladybird shop where our school duffle coats were purchased and where I loved to watch the dancing plastic ladybirds in their tiny mirrored boxes in the front window.

I think the worst feature of the High Row had to be the rickety old bus stands at the bottom tier (which I don't seem to remember giving much shelter at all in the howling winter weather). I'm not sure what they were made of tin, asbestos, corrugated iron but the sheets only seemed to cover the back and the roof leaving the front exposed to the elements, while you waited shivering and freezing for the blue and cream Corporation Bus to turn up.

We would look forward to the Christmas lights being put up, a sure sign that Christmas wouldn't be long, the lights would be strung from one street light to the next along the middle and we would gaze at the window displays in Dressers and Binns. In the summertime we would sit on the benches with an ice-cream and take five minutes out from the busy throng of pushchairs, kids and parents. You were never sat very long before someone you knew would pass by and either nod an 'alright' at you or stop and chat with your mam depending on how well you knew them.

As I grew older the High Row played a different part in my life, it began to be the place where I met my friends as a teenager on a weekend. It was cool to hang around with your latest gear on (bought from the market!) instead of the weekly attire of a school uniform. On a Saturday we would mooch around the shops and market buying a slush puppie and sitting on the High Row, by this time we had progressed to sitting on the railings, as we were of course teenagers and therefore cool. Gradually a group would gather as other friends passed and joined us, however I have to say we did nothing wilder than talk about 'Wham' and never bothered anyone. When my dating days began, again the High Row was there in the background as I kissed a boy for the first time in a heavy, swirling January snowstorm in those same, rickety bus shelters.

As I grew up and married, I pushed my buggies and guided my toddlers down the familiar old Saturday path that my mother had taken me a quarter of a century before. I found it no problem to manoeuvre my buggies through the three tier system and in fact it was somewhat of a Darlington tradition and accepted that you hoiked your buggie onto it's back wheels and bounced it down the steps or walked to one of the three ramps at either end or the middle to get up or down. If you were lucky there was someone around who would give you a lift over those three steps onto the next level.

I am saddened to think my children will never now know my old High Row. It is as I said at the start of this now for me a mere photograph in my mind, but non the less a treasured one.

Elaine Freeman.

Constance's memories

I have lived in Darlington since 1941 and my earliest memories of High Row are between 1942 and 1947 when I lived there, right opposite the Town Clock.

With my parents, who were the caretakers of Martins Bank (now Northern Rock Building Society). Above the bank were the offices of Foster Darling Solicitors and above them was our four bedroomed flat. As you know, the town clock chimes every fifteen minutes but after the first week or so we didn't seem to hear it.

From our sitting room window we had a wide view of High Row, Prebend Row and Tubwell Row. Buses, trams and cars went to and fro, and sometimes tanks rumbled though the town centre. I liked to watch the bus conductors changing the trolleys onto another set of lines, life wasn't half as frantic as it is nowadays.

There were lots of servicemen about, mainly on the High Row I would say. With my friend Jessie, we would lean out of the window to watch them and drop paper pellets, then laugh and wave at those who looked up.

In November of 1943 I started my first job in the office of Binns Ltd. We had to work till 6pm except for half days on Wednesdays. Coming out of the staff entrance in Clarkes Yard then onto High Row many of the girls had boyfriends waiting for them, especially on Friday and Saturday night, to go to the pictures etc..

Also in the evenings High Row was part of a regular promenade around the block of Bondgate, Skinnergate and Post House Wynd, where teenagers would hang about in groups. A group of boys would shout or whistle at passing girls. If you liked the look of them you'd walk around the block and maybe stop and talk, second time around.

Sunday nights, about 7pm, the Salvation Army Band would march from their citadel in Northgate. They would play rousing hymns and preach for about an hour while collecting donations.

Constance Culley.

Footnote from Beryl: What a brilliant place for Constance to have lived in. Those flats on the top of imposing banks and offices have always fascinated me since as a child my family had friends who were caretakers of the Prudential building which used to be in Northgate who used to invite us up there for visits. It was great to look down on the town from such a lofty height and somehow romantic and quirky to know that a family actually lived up there after the workers had gone home. The statue of "Prudentia" was on top of our friends building which made it even more interesting. Constance and her family however had a view over High Row and who could ask for better than that? Hope the chimes of the clock didn't disturb their rest too much, but what a fantastic sight to have outside your window

Mark's memories - My Saturday Memory

Until I was old enough to get a Saturday job, my Saturdays were spent around old High Row sometimes with my parents and my sister. We didn't have much money, but we had lots of love and fun. Our regular Saturday jaunts up and down the High Row are amongst my fondest memories. My sister and I would spend our fifty pence pocket money in that area. We would go down to the outdoor market and look at everything, but I usually would save my pocket money for a treat in Guru...in fact I still do.

Sometimes for a special occasion mum and dad would take us for dinner in the Green Tree Café and I would follow them round with the strange green tray which they piled up with things to eat. Other times for a change we would go to the indoor market and dad would buy us a savoury, which my sister and I would share. Afterwards we would go back along old High Row, happy and tired and I would be reminded not to swing or climb on the railings as we made our way to the bus stop to wait for our bus home.

To this day I visit Darlington and like a pilgrim I wander along High Row remembering my old haunts and the character of the place with happiness tinged with a little sadness for things gone, and the realization that the scene of past memories is no longer there.

Mark Verney.

Old High Row

Tiered steps lead up to iron railings
Framing timeless buildings
Many have stood there watching life
As generations come and go
High Row stood proud
A passer by would feel the same
Hands fast to iron then
Now holding on to memories
Of old High Row.

Mark Verney.

Margaret's memories

As a Darlingtonian I have memories of working in the Green Tree as a Saturday girl when I was sixteen.

At that time the place was thriving, and I asked to make the sandwiches because I wanted to give our customers a good deal. I soon got taken off that job for putting too much filling in the sandwiches! I was made to clear the tables instead.

When I was young traffic was allowed on both the High Row and West Row, as there wasn't much of it then – but now we certainly make up for it with the number of buses that travel through the town centre.

Dad used to be able to park on the High Row and go to the bank, and also one or two more shops nearby. We only had an hour to get as many bits and pieces as we could before a traffic warden came along to hand out parking tickets. Yes, traffic wardens were always around in large numbers in Darlington town centre. At one time parking was allowed in Priestgate, instead of it being a taxi rank, as very few people used to be able to afford taxis.

During my childhood, twenties and thirties Darlington outdoor market used to be flourishing. Fees for market stalls used to be cheap so there were always more market traders wanting a stall in the market place than there were spaces available. There was every type of market stall you could possibly think of, the market place on market days was always jam packed full of customers as well as traders, you sometimes found it difficult making you way between one stall and the next. If you went to Darlington Market on market days you didn't need to go anywhere else to do your shopping, all the food was extremely fresh (twice as fresh as supermarkets and just as cheap) and now Darlington Council have put up the rental of market stalls, a lot of the market traders can no longer afford to make their base there, and that has also meant the loss of a lot of customers to Darlington town centre.

These customers often used other nearby shops, so it has meant a loss of trade to other town centre shops. Shopping centres have been springing up on the outskirts of the town centre with free parking. Town centre parking charges have become so extortionate that customers prefer to shop where it is free parking.

I also have memories of going into the Wimpy Bar not long after I had left school. I have always thought that the Wimpy Bar was a much better version of MacDonalds or Burger King.

I remember My Fair Lady where I used to buy my headscarves and cheap jewellery that looked expensive.
When I was seventeen I saved up my first three months wages to buy the quality black leather jacket I had always wanted from Charles's. Charles sold superior quality clothes and I used to buy all my coats from there.

When I was small my mother bought me all my clothes from the Ladybird shop on the High Row, either there or from Marks & Spencers.

There used to be a really good vegetarian restaurant on the corner of the market place. Although I am not a vegetarian I still enjoy an exciting vegetarian meal for a change.

Binns used to have a good food department which would complement everything sold by the market traders. Mum used to buy freshly ground coffee there – the assistant used to grind the beans for her – where in Darlington can you buy coffee that fresh now? (You could also buy that same coffee from Geoff Wildsmiths in Skinnergate).

I really miss all these small shops we used to have in Darlington where you could get really friendly custom. There are now just a few remaining small shops where you still get friendly shop assistants who care about their customers.

Margaret Greenhalgh.

Footnote From Beryl: Margaret is in poor health at present and so I'm sure we all would like to wish her well

Billy's memories

Writing about the past for people in the future is not an easy thing to do. It all started for me about 58 years ago in our beautiful Victorian market called Darlington where people looked forward to market days on Mondays and Saturdays to try and catch a few bargains. Around six o'clock in the morning the still and quiet of the night came to an end with trolley buses entering the town centre bringing the shift workers to their jobs at Peases Mill. Everything about the town centre was ideal standing looking at the High Row from outside the Kings Head Hotel. You had family businesses like Bainbridge Barkers, Dressers in its old place, then an old shoe shop and Pratts an old family estate agents and possibly solicitors. Then it was the place called Johnson's the cleaners where I had the pleasure to be brought into the world, next to that was, and still is, the beautiful building of the Yorkshire Bank, next was a dress shop called Phillips probably the first childrens Ladybird clothes department stockist in the North East, after that the London and Newcastle grocery store specializing in bacon, cheese and cooked meats. These were all family businesses that weren't caught up in the greed of society, after that Barclays Bank then Lucks the department store which then changed into a new home for Dressers, then Nat West Bank, Dollond & Aitchinsons then a camera shop

Billy Winfield.

(I just love the fact that Billy was born and lived on High Row - that makes two of our contributors who have had the pleasure of dwelling up there above the shopfronts. **Beryl**)

Libby's memories

There has been and will always be High Row in my lifetime, or so I thought until recently.

I remember High Row as a child, and all the individual shops (most of which are now gone). There was, and still is Binns Department Store (I got lost in there when I was very little, which was very scary), where we used to go to get measured for and be bought, new shoes. Then a bit further down was 'Fishy Wilsons' little game shop, and by game I don't mean monopoly or scrabble. He had dead birds, and other dead game, hung up in and around his shop, and there he would be sometimes standing outside, in his white, stained by the tools of his trade apron. I didn't much like that shop at all. I did like Dressers the Stationers, and nearby the 'Ladybird' shop where we used to go to get our chillproof vests for winter, cotton ones for summer and white aertex shirts for games/PE at school, they even sold liberty bodices. As time rolled by some of the smaller shops changed, and so did I. Growing up I went to school followed by college. I got my first car a Renault 4, and got into trouble (well I would have if I'd stopped), on High Row. I can't remember exactly what I did, maybe parked on double yellows, but I was chased down High Row by an irate traffic warden. Luckily I had the advantage of being in a car, even if its top speed wasn't more than a leisurely jog, and I sped away leaving the said warden puffing and panting and glaring after me.

Another memory about High Row, me, and my little red car, came about when I bravely (remember the traffic warden incident), decided to park on High Row briefly as I had to go into one of the shops. In the late 70's as I remember, fake or furry sheepskin type seat covers were quite popular in cars. Someone gave me this yellow one and because it had no ties it used to just sit on my car seat. On this particular day, I had parked up and after doing a quick traffic warden scan, I quickly set off to where I was going. Walking briskly I couldn't help but notice people were staring and giving me odd looks. It took me quite a while to realize what they were looking at.

Horror!! As I looked round I found to my embarrassment a jaundiced looking fury thing hanging out of the waistband of my jeans, as I had been dragging my car seat cover which had caught onto my belt, behind me all the way along High Row. Needless to say I made a quick exit.

These are just a few memories that spring to mind, and I'm sad to say the High Row we knew and loved is now just that, a memory.

Libby.

Stephanie's memories

It seems to me that anyone can remember physical facts. The huge flower troughs and urns of Darlington High Row. The 'Gents' sign leading down a funny smelling staircase to a forbidden underground fault, and so on..

However, it's the personal stuff that makes a collective history so here's mine.
My memories of 'old High Row' are all from the mid 1980's to late 1990's as I'm only twenty six and I left for uni in 1999.

As a child, the Row, along with the covered market, was the mainline artery of the town centre with a heaving stream of bodies, buggies and shopping trolleys. On a Saturday morning it was dog eat dog – you could be subtly edged down from the top to a lower step if you weren't assertive enough. A life lesson there, somewhere!

Now, the buildings. Before part of Barclays Bank was closed for their offices, going there was the highlight of a day's shopping. I chose to open my first bank account there just because it was so lovely – pale stone, almost ecclesiastical archways led into a palace with black and white flawless floors as far as my little eyes could see. Up lit leafy curlicues in the corners of the ceilings seemed to have a significance I wasn't allowed to know. Whilst you waited for your parent to finish their errand, yellow phones were provided for the kids that if picked up, recited soothing stories in Queen's English.

When I was a younger teen, Dressers was my favourite haunt – a mecca of stationery, toys, notebooks, and files for school. Pure, pristine things that made you feel worthy if you bought them. That clean papery smell lingers on in my memory. The art section sold 'Scrape a foils' – black backgrounds where you used a sharp tool to trace a shape of a horse's head, two kittens playing, something equally cute. Aged sixteen when I got an unaccountable taste for Willow Pattern plates and Wedgwood miniatures, the ornament department was heavenly.

When High Row got a Bradford and Bingley Bank the promotional horse and carriage complete with a driver in old fadshioned garb captivated the kids for days.

Then came sixth form. I began my first attempts at fashion and musical tastes. Britpop and faux sixties revival clothes. A friend and I would sit on the uncomfortable wrought iron benches on the lower part, eating Greggs pasties and iced splits, being tormented for scraps by filthy wild pigeons. People would pass who we knew, on the uppermost level, and we'd either smile or suddenly find something, anything, to talk about intently to avoid eye contact!

However, the best thing about the place, which thankfully has been preserved, was that special lofty feeling. You felt as of you were on aloof vantage point. I don't know any other Northern town that has a similar feature. You could see folk coming at you from both directions and people on Low Flaggs who seemed like serfs down there while you assessed the town from on high like some battlemented queen. If you spied someone from afar whom you wanted to avoid, you had a sporting chance of disappearing up one of the Yards before you were clocked. The benevolent Jo Pease at the end was the only one that caught you, and he'd keep your secret.

Stephanie Rickaby.

Faith's memories

Banks and buses
Cars and crowds
Noise and bustle with Mam in tow
My first memories of High Row

The 'Ladybird' shop where I bought my shoes
Along with a scarf I was told not to lose.

Long queues of people waiting at bus stands
Leaning or sitting on the iron balustrades.

Saxone and Dolcis where I bought my first 'heels'
With my first weeks wages - I've forgot how it feels.

Wonderful Dressers who sold pens and ink
Everything useful except kitchen sinks.

The red phone box nearly opposite Barclays
In those heady, exciting 1960's days -
When at seventeen just passed my test
Gladly rang home to make them guess
Dialled their number and button A to press - it was out of order!

The newspaper-seller shouting "Patch"!
Was he calling his dog or meaning Despatch?
For the football results he sold the 'Pink'
If he came back today - what would he think?

Faith Spence.

Joe's memories

Darlington has been my home for all of my life. I'm a Hopetown boy as I grew up there and have kept in contact with that area of the town ever since and for many years was on the committee of Hopetown Working Men's Club. I remember when I was a young lad that Alderman Best used to take a Sunday school at Hopetown mission. I also have had a long association with Darlington's indoor market where I used to work as an errand boy for Ernie Barnett at his fruit and vegetables stall around 1949/1950. My best job at that time was to be sent out for several copies of the 'sporting pink' on a Saturday and then have to distribute them around the market to a lot of the stallholders. The paper cost 2p and for doing this vital job (as everyone wanted to see the football scores), I would get tips of between 3p and even 6p from the grateful market traders. I can well remember that Darlington character Georgie Forbett, his wife Maude and their daughter. George was a familiar figure in town. He was not very tall but everyone knew him and he wore his cap askew in a jaunty manner on his head. He was once jailed for lack of attention to food hygiene, as in the course of his business he would use the same cart to transport fish as he used to transport coal and neglected to clean it out between these two uses. I once had to help him push some goods on a barrow to his house in Freemans Place which was at the bottom of Crown Street. That was a strange old place and no mistake. He had a fire with no back in it and would go and get a grape box or some other handy fuel, and smash it up and light it to make a bonfire in his grate. Another interesting thing about George is the way he carried his cash about. He would cut open the inside of his trouser pocket and attach a pouch on a longish string to the opening of the pocket and then drop the pouch full of money down his trouser leg so that no-one could get at it but him when he hauled it back up to get something out of it. He was a real eccentric. I remember those days with fondness and think the markets, both indoor and outdoor are such an important part of Darlington. I am sorry the outdoor market is no longer on the

Joe with the governess cart -
perhaps he's giving an example to his horse on how to pull it

140

market square as I think that is its home and where it belongs. I've had a full and varied life here in Darlington. I'm married to Sylvia; we have two daughters Tina and Jackie, and are now also grandparents and great grandparents. I also had my own building firm for many years which was hard but worthwhile work. My interests include participating in events at Hopetown club and I am a keen gardener. I have also owned a horse drawn vehicle which I bought from Ray Hankin (the same trap which Guru used in their High Row to High Row competition) and a fine Dales pony named Soames, both myself and my daughter Jackie derived much pleasure from learning to drive him in the trap. We participated in an event to mark the Queen Mother's Jubilee where horse drawn vehicles travelled the length of the country to raise money for various charities.

Joe Watson.

Joe dressed as a Quaker one Christmas at Hopetown Club to sell raffle tickets for good causes

View Across Town

A view of Darlington (with High Row in the distance beneath the town clock), taken from the top floor of Northgate House

Rhythm'n'Blues for Darlington

No-one can complain about the many fantastic (totally free to the public) events which every year are sponsored by Darlington Borough Council. It's not enough to have sponsorship however as what really matters is whether the people running these events know what they are about and that is what makes or breaks an event of any sort. I don't know about all the things that take place as they are many and varied over the year and I don't participate in them all, but I do know there are activities for the very young children in the summer, such as bringing a beach to the market square. There are pop music shows for the teens, and there are tea dances for the older folks. Other happenings which stick in the memory are the Spring Thing when Morris dancers take over the town centre, the winter lantern parade and the Santa Parade (which I'm not sure who pays for but is very festive). The ones I can personally applaud with experience to back me up, are the free fireworks displays every year which always occur on the Saturday nearest to November 5th, and the Darlington Carnival which just gets better every year. My real favourite however being a music person (and one who appreciates nice beer) is the Rhythm'n'Brews festival, which happens in the Arts Centre, the music pubs and Darlington market place every year and which has over the time it has been running featured some amazing line-ups. 2007 was no exception as from Thursday 13th to Sunday 17th of September I counted eighteen bands all of which it would have been a pleasure to see. The culmination of this celebration of The Blues being the Sunday afternoon and evening in the open air on a nice day, in good company, in a fine location, with all the market place pubs and some eateries open for business. The organisers of this proven event also are involved in Darlington Arts Centres R'n'B Club, and as demonstrated by the way they bring such amazing people to this festival year after year really know their stuff so having just found out who these music lovin' individuals are I would like to say thanks to Ian, Bim, Mike, Sue, Malcolm and Phil.

We blues and music aficionados are well catered for in Darlington and vicinity as there are great little clubs all around including the one at Carmel School run by Simon and his friends. Mickleton R'n'B Club

Top Picture - Mike Sanchez
Middle Picture - Oliver Darling
Bottom Picture - Imelda May and Al Gare

142

Beryl, Tony and Colin. The Gurus!

where Sue, Dave and the gang create magical nights every few months and also Guisborough Football Club where a recent triumph for Kath and co was the amazing Ian Siegal. In and around Darlington there is a good pub, club and music scene, in fact too many good venues to list but The Forum in Borough Road must get a mention, and there are many more...

There have also been lots of great bands in and around Darlington such as The Rye and The Jaded, to name but two... All in all this is a town which revels in all genres of music from popular, rock, punk, indie right through to classical. We even had the great Jimi Hendrix at the Imperial many years ago...

Tracy, Gary and Family

Sophie and Lliam
(aka Elvis)

Emilio, Colin, Helen, Harley and Bandit

Chris Farlowe and The Norman Beaker Band who apart from headlining the 2007 Rhythm'n'Brews Festival in Darlington Market Place recently made a triumphant return to Newcastle (where Chris 'cut his teeth' at the legendary 'Club a Gogo'), and both Chris and Norman have partaken in good humoured collaborations over the years with Van Morrison

Darlington enjoys an excellent council sponsored Blues Festival every year featuring many wonderful blues musicians and plenty of good beer too. These have been just a few of the cool people who have been here

Having fun
In Darlington
Can often be totally free
Even if not
I don't give a jot
As this is the place to be.

Beryl

Ian Siegal and his brilliant band once played Darlington. This man is so devilishly great and so steeped in music that when you hear him it's like a light has been switched on

Time for Santa

We would like to mention here George Harrison who was our good friend and also was an excellent Santa for Guru for many years and was much liked and well received as he distributed gifts in Darlington.

The Santa Parade comes to Darlington every year before Christmas and snow, hail, rain or building works it never stops families from lining the streets to welcome Santa and his adorable reindeer!

Coming up on page 147 you'll see a humourous incident on High Row described - well this is Beryl (in the red coat concerned) and her friend Valerie (minus specs), posing with Santa at the town clock immediately after the incident took place!

Humorous High Row

It's refreshing when we don't take things too seriously, so a little innocent irreverence or wonder never hurt anyone... and can raise a smile!

Untitled Anecdote...

My fondest memories of the High Row are from 1974 when I was sixteen, gorgeous and had a figure to die for. My mother had bought me a grey wool pencil-skirt, which was so close fitting it looked like body art. The skirt was quite long and had no split to allow for movement. On my first visit to town in my new suit, I felt like a glamorous 1950's film star. I wiggled my way up to the High Row steps, only to find that my legs were so tightly bound in that skirt that I couldn't get up them.

I also remember that it was around that time my elder sister told me about 'Pease's Widger'. She said that if you stood outside the Gas Board and looked at the statue, you could see it in all it's glory. I was disappointed to find that it was actually his pocket watch, but I still find it funny today. I took my mum to see it for the first time recently, though obviously since the statue's relocation it's no longer visible from High Row, which seems a shame. It can now be seen from the new paved area, somewhere between the end of the steps and the HSBC bank.

Sue Cummings.

Young love on old High Row

High Row , in my youth, was always the place to meet friends before going on a night out. It was there that I met my husband of 33 years. Saturday 16 May, 1970. I was in town with my friend, he was in town with his friend, my friend knew his and as they stood there talking on High Row, near what now must be Peters Bakery, but was then I think Jean Jungle, we got talking as well. I remember that there was music, Band of Gold by Freda Payne, playing in the Jeans shop. Next night at the Flamingo Club disco we met again and that was it. After that we regularly met outside Dolcis further along High Row and we often caught the last no 2B bus home from there too. No High Row - no marriage. It has a lot to answer for!

Francis Robinson.

More snippets and anecdotes!

I had arranged to meet my very attractive but short-sighted friend on High Row and I was a bit late. It was the early sixties I had jet black bouffant hair and I was dressed in my usual bright red funnel necked swing backed winter coat (it was the only decent coat I had). I'd just passed the town clock when I saw her standing there waiting, and as I ran up the steps to join her I realised she was speaking but I couldn't see who to. "Hey Valerie, sorry I'm late" I called out "you're surely not talking to yourself are you?" She swung round looking embarrassed and said "if that's you Beryl who have I been chattering to?" We then both suddenly realised that not having her glasses on she had mistaken the big round red post box with the black top on High Row for me…we had a good laugh at that, and agreed that either me going on a diet or her wearing her glasses all the time would maybe help prevent it happening again.
Beryl.

Once I dreamed that I was on High Row near the Binns end and Robbie Williams was at the other end nearer the monument…as we both neared Post House Wynd we saw each other, our eyes met and we began to run towards each other like Kathy and Heathcliffe did in that scene on the moors from Wuthering Heights…then I woke up!
Anon.

Oh, she'll tak' the High Row, and I'll tak' Prebend Row,
And she'll be in Northgate afore me.
But me and my true love will never meet again,
'cos I'm stuck at the top of Priestgate, waiting for a gap between the buses and taxis!
Keith Pybus.

Many years ago way back in the very early fifties the Co-op Hall in Priestgate was very popular for dancing. one evening I was dancing with a gentleman when he uttered "Is the perfume you are wearing 'Evening in Paris' or 'Saturday night on the High Row?' Evening in Paris perfume was popular at the time.
Doreen Turner (nee Hodgson).

I am pleased I was born in 1919 and had all the happy times that I spent in Darlington. It was the best place in all England. It was always busy, people came from far and near. Well I hope they will again for the shops and the market. For me it is not the same old happy town it was, but I hope the young people will enjoy it as much as I have.
Betty Inns (Mrs).

Where is the Quaker town
Of which we were taught,
Has it been sold and bought?
Where are the railings which were such fun,
To swing upon when we were young?
Our market place was bustling then,
and market traders had more cash,
I am still young but miss the past
When simple things were made to last
Oh where are those railings
I used to swing on when I was young,
Where is my Quaker town?
Marian Bell.

"Now the famous High Row is no more
We have had lots of rain to pour
Now it's sort of levelled off
That's the end of being a Toff"
Elsie Pescod.

Tony "being a Toff"

Epitaph for the Old High Row

The market clock looks down
upon the town.
Impervious to time, it flicks the years
away with thin, cold hands.
It neither knows nor cares
of change, nor marks the steep
white steps, the hard dark slabs
that hold the twisting evergreens,
the simple flowers
it only tells the hours.

Pehaps we will forget
the old High Row. Photographs
can show a Darlington now past.
From his refurbished plinth
the Quaker Pease will gaze
with sightless eyes,
revealing what is lost.

Rosemary Sandford.

The Judges - Allene

One of our judges.

Allene Norris has had successful careers in journalism, broadcasting and lately as an author of several popular books including the best selling 'Grannies like us' inspired by being an adoring and adored grandmother.

Allene said...

"What a difficult task! There were some marvellously written pieces from people of all ages and from all walks of life. What pleased me most as a judge was that there were quite a few entries from men, indeed two of my prize-winners are men.

There were so many that nearly made it; the ghost story, which I suppose really was "the spirit" of High Row; a piece about the A1 running through Darlington; the ones about the magic of Christmas Eve in the town centre and so many more. There was plenty of humour, some first class poetry and some very short entries.

One or two entries were anonymous and I particularly liked the one from someone who bemoaned having to move to Darlington and then saw the High Row and the beautiful clock tower and has loved living here ever since. The late Yvonne Talbot, who illustrated my market book, way back in the 1980's felt the same when she moved here from the south, but then was overwhelmed by the beauty of the High Row, our handsome clock, the indoor market and the friendly traders there.

It took me a long time to scrutinise the many enjoyable and fine entries, but winners there had to be, so the words in the title of this book "spirit of High Row" was taken into account and so too the writing ability involved. The entire competition has proved to me, what an affection people have for Darlington and its High Row…the latter truly the heart of the town. I wish this book much success for it deserves it".

Allene Norris

Here are Allene's reasons for her three equal top choices:

High Row Christmas Eve 1972 by Martin A Conway warmed my heart. It was so natural. I loved the "loose" writing (not unlike descriptive Dylan Thomas!), the lads meeting up and the High Row being commonplace to them. You could imagine the young macho northern mates, then suddenly after the tough image, an unexpected snow-storm stirs a human emotion within, where the sheer joy and exuberance of it, brings out the childlike innocence once more. That moment must have been very special for it is remembered so affectionately thirty years later.

'Atkinson & Co' is just a heavenly chunk of Darlington's history told remarkably to her neighbour (Mrs Dulcie Noble), by a woman who is already in her nineties. This entry has a wealth of detail about our beloved town that many will recognise and those who do not should enjoy reading about. She recalls her family connections to the High Row and the very up-market shop there. Who else knew that the huge top hat outside the shop was painted grey during the Second World War to blend in with the buildings and so detract enemy war planes from bombing it? There's a wonderful human memory here from the former Miss Atkinson, now Joan Wright.

On High Row by Ian C Rutland, I have chosen for its simplicity. After all, in almost every entry there is a mention of the High Row being a place to promenade, but most of all a meeting place. The poem, tells of the youthful agony of waiting for a special person and the ecstasy. The writer has obviously written this from personal experience, and I loved the last line "…I'm glad you waited"

I wonder what happened next?

Martin A Conway '**High Row Christmas Eve 1972**'.
Joan Wright '**Atkinson & Co**'.
Ian C Rutland '**On High Row!**'.

The judges - Richard

One of our judges.

Richard Hindle has Darlington art gallery Gallerina and excels in making modern art accessible to everybody.

Richard said...

"What an honour to be asked to share in the memories and creations of so many. While so personal to all of those who have taken the time to write and send images, they seem at the same time so familiar to all who have been allowed to share this same stage whilst each of us tell our own story, some of simple or indeed magical shopping trips, whilst others waited and waited, met and fell in love.

Happy, sad, abstract and eloquent, how wonderful that each of us have made special this one part of our town's unique heritage – an important realisation too that these words are from and about this town's people, a reminder perhaps that this 'pedestrian heart' lies not on the ground cut from granite, but that the heart of this town is its people who will continue to colour, compliment and contrast and move forward with its ever changing surroundings".

Richard Hindle.

Richard chose as his winners:
David Thompson '**Spirits in the Stones**'.
Scott Rollo '**I took my girl to Darlington**'.
Maureen Snowball '**The High Row legend of Pease and the Town Clock**'.

The judges - Tony

One of our judges.

Tony Smith studied history at York University from 1973 to 1975 and since then (in spite of the story that follows), has chosen to be part of the fulfilling madness which is Guru Boutique.

The incident of the 'bunny rabbit' t shirt by Tony Smith.

Once upon a time in the early 1970's when I was an innocent young man not long left grammar school I decided to take a part time job in the cellar bar of the Bowes public house, the side entrance to which was in Mechanics Yard. Not having many clothes which were suitable for such an establishment I went to see my friend Beryl and her mother Mrs Maughan in Guru in the Court Arcade. "I'll fix you up Tony" said Beryl cheerfully, and proceeded to sell me a pair of purple loon pants, a belt with a little leather pouch attached to it, and worst of all a flared sleeved, scoop necked t shirt with what resembled two ladies boobs and some bunny rabbits embroidered on it. More like 'stitched me up' I think! Beryl assured me that the animals embroidered on my top were antelope not rabbits and like the fool I was I believed her, and started my new job down in the cellar bar of the pub wearing this ensemble. I was soon to find out that my apparel became a source of amusement to the biker clientele who frequented the Bowes at that time. One evening trying to be diligent at my work it got to past closing time and no-one seemed inclined to leave. After a few hints to all assembled I finally summoned up the courage to very firmly rap on the bar and say at the top of my voice "get your drinks off please it's after closing time". The place went deadly silent and to my horror the largest of the bikers, I think his name was Chewbacca, stood up and came towards me pint in hand. His huge hairy arm slowly but surely positioned the almost full glass above me and then he very carefully poured the lot over my head. Not knowing what the best action to take would be I simply wiped my eyes with the bar towel and looked him in the eye and whispered "thank you". With sneering looks in my direction the bikers then all trooped out and I breathed a sigh of relief. After all it was probably all my fault for letting someone talk me into wearing a 'bunny rabbit' t shirt, as how could I command respect wearing that. The t shirt was ruined as all the colours ran into one another after the soaking it had received so it was never worn again. Chewbacca had unintentionally done me a big favour.

Tony says...

"I had supposed that working at Guru in the centre of Darlington for so long would sort of qualify me to recognise which of the contributions stood out amongst all those received for this book. However I found all the work submitted was outstanding and it was with great difficulty that I finally narrowed my choice down to these four which receive the special Guru award for putting a different slant on their chosen subject".

Tony Smith

Marion Watson for 'The other side of the window' as she tells us about High Row from a completely different viewpoint.

Sylvia Gargett for 'Memories of Darlington High Row' a fine piece of descriptive prose which makes us proud to be Darlingtonians.

Mary Burnside for 'Tales of High Row' which touched our hearts and shows awareness of others.

Sue Cummins for the irreverently innocent 'untitled anecdote' she sent in which made us smile.

Family Album

In Loving memory of
Rupert Maughan (1917-2002)
Helen Irene Maughan (nee Fishburn) (1920-2005)
George Humphrey Johnston Fishburn (1917 -2006)
and others no longer with us, who we miss

The lives of these exceptional people epitomise the qualities of the era they lived in,
and they had the ability to adapt and survive and touch the lives of others
in a positive way in an ever changing world.

These names are added in order to show
how fondly remembered are the people and places we truly care for.

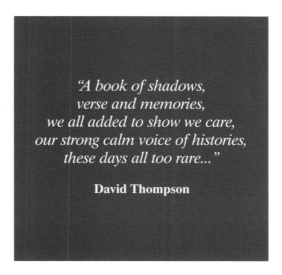

"A book of shadows,
verse and memories,
we all added to show we care,
our strong calm voice of histories,
these days all too rare..."

David Thompson

What follows are some photographs from the days of sepia and black & white...

People of the early High Row era!

The lives of these family members of mine stretch right across the whole of the time that Darlingons High Row was in existance. The eldest of them being born well before 1901 when it first began to serve Darlington and the youngest being still very much here in 2007 to witness its demise. I'm sure many of you reading this will remember your own fantastic family members of the same era.

George Maughan loved music and always had two old gramophones with horns for amplification and scratchy needles. He liked to keep a spare in case one broke down!

My great gran Sarah Susannah and her baby Barbara Maughan who grew up to be a talanted pianist and my grandma. She lived in a tiny village called Burril near Bedale but liked to make the journey to the town of Darlington. Sarah Susannah was a beautiful Victorian lady with a complexion like peaches and cream. She always wore a high collar embellished with a brooch.

Annie Fishburn made the transition from Victorian girl to modern woman being one of the first lady drivers of her time when she bought a car to replace the horse and cart she used to transport churns of milk from farm to market with. She ran a red traffic light in Stockton because she had never seen one before and didn't know what it was!

Sarah's son George Maughan with my dad Rupert. George loved the Music Hall and was a frequent visitor to Darlington where he would be seen strutting proudly down High Row wearing spats before going to a show at The Astoria or The Hippodrome.

Helen Irene Fishburn.
('Little Miss Fishbone') as
Rupert (my dad) used to call her.

Rupert Maugham (Rupe) who
had just joined the Scottish regiment
the Black Watch came a courting.
Irene and Rupe met at Eppelby
Gala. He wore his kilt for the
village dance and all the local girls
tried to get a peek as he twirled
around the floor with Irene.

Tom and Annie Fishburn. Tennant
farmers at Kirkby Malzeard, then
Picton, then Middleton St George.
This was taken outside their house in
Hudson Terrace, MSG, with little
Irene and Humphrey (Slasher)
Fishburn. Note Annies fashionable
bob haircut, which is very different from
her former long auburn locks. She once
ran all the way from Middleton St
George to Darlington pushing little
Irene in her pushchair, who had been
accidentally injured in the eye by a gun
cartridge, to their doctor in Coniscliffe
Road.

Rupert was extremely handsome and
Irene was totally in love with him.
He had been a cadet, had joined the
Black Watch and got Tom
Fishburn to buy him out. He married
Irene after they had tried
unsuccessfully to elope and he then
joined the Green Howards.

Irene and Rupert – Theirs was a
stormy but true love affair which
lasted right through their 63 years of
marriage. Irene was strong and
steadfast right to the end.

Irene and Humph. Two wonderful
people and a brother and sister who
went the extra mile for each other.
When Irene had to have a thyroid
operation when she was 21,
Humphrey who had given up on
following his father Tom into farming
and now worked for Tom Cracknell's
haulage firm worked to pay for her
operation which saved her life.

Irene and Humphrey were once left
alone while Tom and Annie went out.
They found the rhubarb wine and
when their parents returned they found
Irene playing the piano with her bare
toes.

Humphrey was a strong willed boy
and when his teacher told him to go and
stand in a corner because he was a
dunce, he grabbed her cane out of her
hand, swung its handle round her neck
and dragged her round the classroom.
He left school early needless to say.

Rupert (Bob) Maughan.
The life and soul of every party and
my dad.

Humph was swept off his feet in Darlington by an extremely 'modern' miss named
Doris French. Doris was smart, striking to look at and highly intelligent. She was
working as a lady taxi driver (very daring for those times) and they met when she picked
him up in her taxi from the pub that used to stand near Stone Bridge. They arranged to
meet at the Civic Theatre on a cold September night. Their love must have kept them
warm as from that first date they were inseperable and were married exactly six weeks
from meeting one another. L to R: Mr French (Doris's father), Rupert Maughan
(my dad), Humphrey Fishburn (the groom), Doris French (now Fishburn), Sylvia
French (Doris's sister), Tom Fishburn (my grandad and Humphrey's & Irene's
dad), a family friend and seated in front Irene Maughan (with me on her knee),
Annie Fishburn (my nana and Humph & Irenes mother).

Three generations. Annie, Irene and Beryl. My beautiful mam was a rock to all of us and so loving and lovely.

Meet Rupert's side of the family - L to R: Gorgeous uncle Roland (Rupert's step brother), Barbara Tanner (Rupert's step sister and ex chorus girl), nana Tanner, Irene, Clarence (Rupert's stepbrother), Front Row: Aunty Minnie, Aunty Maureen, David Tanner?, and me. (Aunty Minnie is the nicest of ladies, and it was uncle Roland and lovely Aunty Maureen who were to take me on a memorable Christmas trip to High Row which is detailed in this book. This was taken on our one and only holiday, a weekend in a caravan (that leaked gas from its cooking facility), on a site in Redcar. I loved every minute.

Young Raymond Hankin, at school in Bishop Auckland.
Ray and I had yet to meet when these photo's were taken but just a few years later the High Row was to be the venue for our first peck on the cheek which eventually led to marriage in 1963.

I don't regret the emotion in this as I love all these people in different ways - especially Irene (my mam). Many of these excellent and interesting people are no longer wih us but all of them really knew how to live and cope in a era which was full of people of great character, standards and determination. They all shared a great love of Darlington and although the older ones amongst them originally lived outside the town they all gravitated to this place and some came to live here whilst others were frequent visitors and all of them have graced our old High Row. I'm sorry I don't have any photographs or memories of readers beloved family members of the era to put on this page but at least we may remember them as this little story has hopefully sparked off many memories.

Epilogue

Real hometowns like real families engender love and loyalty and don't conform to a formula. Therefore it seems right that if changes that threaten the identity of a place are deemed to be necessary, the form those changes will take should start from the viewpoint of the people involved who (as one of our contributors David Thompson so rightly said), are the true "guardians" of the public places they inhabit. Change which profoundly affects people's lives usually causes strong feelings in hearts and minds, so a lot of care should be applied before final decisions involving environment are made, as once cherished sites such as our former High Row are gone, they are gone forever, and all that they meant to people is gone with them.

There was controversy when the old High Row was constructed on the then familiar wide featureless space, which stretched between High Row and West Row, but it was a necessary undertaking to cope with the increased traffic flowing through the town. It turned out to be a good decision to build it, and it served us well and safely right up to the day it was bulldozed away, and even if it was no longer fulfilling its original purpose had become quite a tourist attraction in our town.

There is controversy now about what we have in its place. Does it fit in with the remaining historical buildings and areas surrounding it in the town? Does it say loudly and proudly 'this is Darlington'? Will it stand up to the ravages of use to become a future classic in its own right? We all may have our own views but only time will tell the outcome of this slanted, two tiered thoroughfare which has replaced its three tiered predecessor. How people react to the appearance and use of anything is always going to be subjective anyway, but one thing is certain this new High Row has a hard act to follow.

Darlington deserves much commercial success as not only does it combine the best of both worlds in many ways…traditional markets and modern shopping experiences…but more than that it is 'our' town, full of the landmarks, characters, quirks and contradictions, and the myriad of memories and experiences whether they be bad or good, sad or funny, that make a place human and complete. We have tried to put some of that variety into this book. Where else could you find references to punks and bikers, or reminiscences of 'Dragonites', right next to wonderfully individual historical insights, poignant family stories and uniquely descriptive memories?

The essence of old High Row was perhaps, a powerful combination of two elements spiritual and physical, and I agree with what our judges seem to convey with regard to this idea in their summaries. I think I know what Richard means when he says "this 'pedestrian heart' lies not on the ground cut from granite, but in its people". I concur with Allene when she remarks on how much affection people have for Darlington, and describes the physical entity known as High Row as "truly the heart of the town".

I feel that the people featured, and the things they have shared with us in regard to old High Row, may have combined here to give a true reflection of Darlington's heart and soul. I sincerely hope so anyway. Sincere gratitude goes to all involved in 'That Darlington Way' in any capacity whatsoever, for sharing in the obvious affection we had for old High Row and which we still have for our town. For my part to have been able to provide a vehicle in which people could articulate their own take on old High Row has taken a heavy toll on me and six months out of my life, but it was a necessary compulsion in order to do right by that place. To me the loss of 'my High Row' is somehow inextricably linked with the loss of my own loved ones, as I did so much which involved them in the vicinity of High Row and now I can no longer have the comfort of being able to picture these much loved relatives there. So you see it's partly a general sadness I feel for the demise of part of the town's history, and partly a personal sorrow which leaves me feeling as though I have had my roots pulled up from underneath me. Whilst I know that we can do no more now as it is truly the end of an era for the town, in spite of my own dismay I wish the 'new' Darlington nothing but luck for the future, as this is also the start of a new era albeit one which yet has to prove itself. Darlington is an excellent town which deserves to be loved, and I would never want it to come to harm however disappointed I myself may feel. I really hope that between us all we have produced a valuable publication, (because if not the two and a half stones of weight I have put on due to scoffing all those packets of chocolate digestive biscuits in the early hours of many, many mornings whilst compiling it will have been a needless sacrifice).

P.S. Some student journalists recently asked me which three words I would use to describe Darlington before the changes and straight away I said "my home town", then they asked which three words would describe how I felt about Darlington now and my answer had to be "I feel lost". Perhaps this uprooted feeling is partly what made me embark upon this task of celebrating High Row. Getting immersed in writing my own bits and putting such intense thought and energy into compiling the fantastic works of all the contributors to 'That Darlington Way' has not saved me from a nervous breakdown brought on by my sense of loss, it IS my nervous breakdown, as if I hadn't poured my fierce love of this town and its people into this book I really don't know what would have happened to me.

Thank you for sharing it all.

B.H.

Photo supplied by Bridget Emmerson from her collection of Prudhoes postcards.

Ordering and contact details

If you would like to order further copies of this book, or have any comments you would like to make about it, we would love to hear from you. We can be contacted at any of the addresses, telephone numbers and websites listed below.

The cost of the book is £12.99 plus £2 postage & packing.
We accept credit cards, or cheques payable to Guru Boutique and sent to

Guru Boutique,
24 Blackwellgate,
Darlington,
DL1 5HG.

Tel: 01325461479 (office hours).
Email: darlophile63@yahoo.co.uk
MySpace: www.myspace.com/gurudarlington   and   www.myspace.com/aboutdarlington
Web address: www.gurudarlington.co.uk

The book will be available for sale in Guru, from our website or you could order by letter or telephone from the address and telephone number above
(please include full contact details whichever method you use).

'That Darlington Way' will also be available from Amazon and to order from all good bookshops.